Lee Canter's

ASSERTIVE DISCIPLINE®
Secondary Workbook

Grades 6–12

Solution Tree

D0814022

Cover Design by Christine Tysowsky

Text design by Carolyn Wendt and Bob Winberry

Illustrations by Patty Briles and Jane Yamada

Printed in the United States of America

ISBN 1-932127-48-8

Contents

Preface

Assertive Discipline is a highly regarded classroom behavior management program that was first developed in 1976. Over time, the program has evolved to meet the changing needs of today's classrooms. The focus of the Assertive Discipline program is on teaching students to assume responsibility for their own behavior. With this proactive and preventive approach, teachers can go beyond establishing basic discipline in their classrooms to creating cooperative environments in which students learn to choose appropriate, responsible behavior.

This *Assertive Discipline Secondary Workbook* is your guide to implementing the Assertive Discipline program, as described in the book *Assertive Discipline: Positive Behavior Management for Today's Classroom, 3rd Edition.* The easy-to-follow format presents brief overviews of the program's key points, as well as reproducible forms, positive notes, bookmarks, coupons, raffle tickets, tracking sheets, communication and documentation pages, and visual aids that will allow you to successfully integrate the program into your teaching routine.

This book is intended for use by any teacher who teaches multiple classes. The use of the word *secondary* is meant to include both middle school and high school teachers. There are a variety of suggestions and reproducibles so that you may choose the ones most suitable to the grade level and maturity of your students.

Introduction

The job of a teacher is challenging—especially in today's world. You may find, like many teachers today, that it is increasingly difficult to establish a classroom environment free from disruptive behavior. But in spite of the difficulties you face, you can create and maintain the kind of classroom in which you can effectively teach and your students can learn and grow academically and socially.

How can you achieve this? By approaching the management of classroom behavior in a proactive manner. Whatever the age of your students, they will behave more responsibly and have more success at school if you give as much thought and planning to behavior management as you do to any instructional or curriculum practice. To become more proactive, you will want to follow these guidelines:

➤ Build positive, trusting relationships with your students by establishing yourself as a teacher who cares about their well-being in and out of school.

➤ Establish rules and specific directions that clearly define the limits of acceptable and unacceptable student behavior.

➤ Teach your students to consistently follow these rules and directions—to choose to behave responsibly—throughout the school day and the school year.

➤ Provide students with consistent recognition when they do behave. Adolescents are eager for your positive words of encouragement and support, even if they don't always show it.

➤ Adopt a positive, assertive manner when responding to students. Students trust and respect the calm, consistent, and caring presence of an assertive teacher. They know that the teacher has a set of limits and that he or she will follow through appropriately whenever a student chooses not to behave. There is no confusion, no second guessing, no hostility, no anger.

➤ Remember to ask parents and administrators for their assistance when their support is needed. You can't do it alone. Education is a cooperative effort between teacher, student, parents, and administration. Rely on each other for the positive assistance you can give.

Help your students make the most of their middle school and high school years. Create an atmosphere in which student self-esteem can flourish and you can feel accomplished at the end of every day. Become a positive, proactive teacher—today!

Your Classroom Discipline Plan

In this section of the *Assertive Discipline Secondary Workbook,* we will first look at the classroom discipline plan—what it is and how it empowers secondary students to become responsible for their behavior choices. Then you will develop a discipline plan for your own classroom with rules, supportive feedback, and corrective actions that best fit your needs and the needs of your students.

Also included in this section are a wide variety of reproducibles that will help you successfully develop and implement your classroom discipline plan.

What Is a Classroom Discipline Plan?

A classroom discipline plan is a system that allows you to spell out the behaviors you expect from students and what they can expect from you in return. The plan provides a framework around which all your classroom behavior management efforts can be organized.

The goal of a classroom discipline plan is to have a fair and consistent way to establish a safe, orderly, positive classroom environment in which you can teach and students can learn.

A classroom discipline plan consists of three parts:

➤ **RULES** that students must follow at all times

➤ **SUPPORTIVE FEEDBACK** that students will receive for following the rules

➤ **CORRECTIVE ACTIONS** that you will use when students choose not to follow the rules

Here is a sample classroom discipline plan for a secondary classroom:

CLASSROOM RULES
Follow directions.
Be in the classroom and seated when the bell rings.
Use appropriate language; no put downs or teasing.

SUPPORTIVE FEEDBACK
Verbal recognition
Individual rewards, such as:
    Positive notes sent home to parents
    Positive phone calls to parents
    Privilege pass
Classwide rewards

CORRECTIVE ACTIONS

First time a student breaks a rule:	Reminder
Second time:	Stay in class one minute after the bell, or change seat for remainder of period
Third time:	Stay in class two minutes after bell
Fourth time:	Teacher calls parents
Fifth time:	Send to administrator
Severe clause:	Send to administrator

If students are to learn the self-discipline that is so crucial to their success in school, and to their success in life, they must first understand exactly what is expected of them.

Look at it this way: In the workplace, employees are given precise job descriptions and clear explanations of all policies that affect their performance. Only if expectations are clarified can performance be fairly and accurately evaluated.

It is important, therefore, to have a classroom management structure in place that clearly indicates limits and boundaries.

Below are five reasons why a classroom discipline plan will help you create a positive learning environment in your classroom that benefits both you and your students.

Benefits of a Classroom Discipline Plan

1. A discipline plan makes managing student behavior easier.

Planning is the key to successful classroom management. When you have a plan for how you will respond to student behavior, you won't have to make on-the-spot decisions about what to do when a student misbehaves—or how to properly recognize a student who does behave appropriately. You will know what to do, your students will know what to expect, and the guesswork (and stress) will be eliminated from your daily disciplinary efforts.

A plan also provides the basis for teaching self-management. When the system for

required school behavior is taught up front to the class, students then have the responsibility to use self-control and make good choices.

2. A discipline plan protects students' rights.

All students have rights to the same due process in the classroom. A discipline plan will help ensure that you deal with each student in a fair and consistent manner—a fact that plays into the middle school and high school student's sense of fairness.

Likewise, the classroom discipline plan protects students' right to learn. Most students want to learn and hate having their time wasted by a few.

3. A discipline plan helps ensure safety for all students in the classroom.

Consistently used as part of a teacher's behavior management efforts, a classroom discipline plan helps reduce behavior problems in class. And reduced behavior problems means a safer environment for all students. This is extremely important. Secondary students do not want to be placed in the position of having the "tough" kids running the class.

4. A discipline plan increases the likelihood of parental support.

When you communicate your discipline plan to parents, you are letting them know that you care about guiding their children toward making responsible behavioral choices. This is a powerful message of support and professionalism to give to parents.

5. A discipline plan helps ensure administrator support.

A discipline plan demonstrates to your administrator (dean, counselor, principal, or vice principal) that you have a well-thought-out course of action for managing student behavior in your classroom. When your administrator understands the commitment you've made to effective classroom management, you will be better able to get support when you need it.

 It's Your Turn

Now we'll take you through the steps of creating a classroom discipline plan that is tailor-made for you and your students.

First, you will plan the general rules for your classroom.

Second, you will choose the supportive feedback you will use to motivate students to follow those rules.

Finally, you will learn how to most effectively correct students' behavior when they are not following the rules.

Option: Form a Behavior Management Team

To best meet the needs of your students, and to minimize confusion over varying expectations from teacher to teacher, collaborate with a few other teachers to develop a common classroom discipline plan. The team can be formed in a variety of ways. If you are part of an interdisciplinary team whose individual members teach the same students, this team can develop a common plan. You may also form a Behavior Management Team with several teachers in your section of the building or with teachers who teach some of the same students (e.g., ninth-grade teachers). Students will become more cooperative as they find that expectations are consistent from classroom to classroom. The more consistency provided within the school, the easier your job will be.

After formulating the plan, meet with your team once or twice during the quarter or semester to evaluate the effectiveness of the plan and make any changes necessary.

Creating Your Classroom Discipline Plan
Rules

Teachers at the secondary levels sometimes assume that students should automatically know how to behave in the classroom. They expect that after numerous years in school, a student should understand the general expectations of the classroom.

This assumption is often erroneous. Whether seventh-graders or twelfth-graders, your students all share something in common when they arrive in your class—each brings a variety of behavioral expectations from previous teachers and schools.

In addition, different teaching styles and curriculum needs result in different behavioral expectations in secondary school classes.

Your students can't be expected to know how *you* want them to behave in *your* classroom unless you make these expectations clear to them. General classroom rules, therefore, are the first part of your classroom discipline plan.

What are general classroom rules?

General classroom rules are those rules that are in place all day long—throughout all activities. General classroom rules are important because they let your students know what basic behavioral expectations you have at all times.

These guidelines will help you choose appropriate rules.

Choose rules that are observable and continually in effect.

Address behaviors that you can clearly see. Vaguely stated expectations may mean one thing to one student and an entirely different thing to another. As a result, they often cause problems by opening the doors to arguments regarding interpretation.

For example:

Observable Rules
➤ Keep hands and feet to yourself.

➤ Be in your seat when the bell rings.

➤ No yelling.

Vague Expectations
➤ Respect teacher and fellow students.

➤ No fooling around when class starts.

➤ No unnecessary talking.

Choose rules that apply throughout the period.

General classroom rules are rules that apply all period, no matter what activity is taking place. These are rules that students are expected to follow at all times.

Choose a limited number of classroom rules.

Three to five general classroom rules are plenty. The more rules you have, the more difficult it will be for students to remember them. Choose the ones you most need so that you can teach and your students can learn.

Now, before you choose your own rules, take a look below at some rules that are *not* appropriate general classroom rules. Though often seen in classrooms, we have found that these rules are not appropriate general classroom rules because they are not applicable throughout the period. Notice that while each rule *sounds* sensible, it cannot be a realistic ongoing expectation.

Rules to Avoid

• **Raise your hand and wait to be called on before you speak.**
There are going to be times when students are expected to speak out (for example, during group work or in certain whole-class discussions). Also, you may not want to put yourself in the position of having to provide a corrective action for what might simply be a student's overly enthusiastic behavior.

• **Stay in your seat unless you have permission to get up.**
There may be many times during the period when it is OK for a student to get up without asking permission. Again, this rule may not be enforceable throughout the class period.

• **Complete all homework assignments.**
This rule does not relate to classroom behavior, and there may be times when completing homework is out of a student's control.

When you establish general classroom rules that do not clearly reflect your consistent expectations, you run the risk of confusing students, and you will not be able to enforce these rules with consistency.

General Classroom Rules Appropriate for Students in Grades 6–12

Notice that each of these rules is applicable every day—throughout the entire class period.

➤ Follow directions.

➤ Keep hands to yourself.

➤ Do not leave the room without permission.

➤ No swearing, teasing, or yelling.

➤ Be in your seat when the bell rings.

➤ Don't interrupt when someone else is speaking.

Involve students in choosing rules for the classroom.

Many teachers find it beneficial to involve their students in choosing the general rules for the classroom. You might begin by presenting an analogy that helps explain why clearly defined rules are a smart idea: What if driving laws (rules) simply consisted of the admonition to "drive friendly"? What would be the effect in comparison to having clear-cut, carefully spelled-out laws?

Then, during a brief class discussion, ask students to consider how other students sometimes make it difficult for them to pay attention and learn in class. Ask for suggestions for rules that might make it easier to learn.

During the discussion, guide students so that suggested rules are both appropriate and realistic. Consider student input, but be sure that the final rules you choose follow the guidelines given and also follow your own needs as a teacher.

By including students in the process of choosing rules, you will give them ownership in the classroom discipline plan. They will see the classroom rules as their rules (with a rationale that makes sense to them) and will be more motivated to support and remind each other about following the rules.

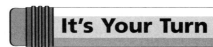

It's Your Turn

Use the Classroom Rules Worksheet on the next page to plan the general classroom rules you will use in your own classroom. When you're finished, enlarge the Classroom Rules poster on page 13 and write your rules on it.

CLASSROOM RULES WORKSHEET

Use this worksheet to plan your own general classroom rules. We've started the list for you with the rule "Follow directions." This is important because students must be expected to follow any directions you might give during the day. When choosing the rest of your rules, remember: 1) rules must be observable; 2) rules must apply throughout the entire day; and 3) rules must reflect your teaching style and educational philosophy.

Classroom Rule: Follow directions.

This is an appropriate rule because:

_____

_____

_____

_____

Classroom Rule: _____

This is appropriate because:

_____

_____

_____

_____

Classroom Rule: _____

This is appropriate because:

_____

_____

_____

_____

Classroom Rule: _____

This is appropriate because:

_____

_____

_____

_____

CLASSROOM
★ *Rules* ★

Creating Your Classroom Discipline Plan
Supportive Feedback

Your general classroom rules are the first part of your classroom discipline plan. The second part of your classroom discipline plan, supportive feedback, will help you motivate your students to follow these rules.

Supportive feedback is the sincere and meaningful attention you give a student for meeting your expectations—for choosing responsible behavior that will lead to greater success in school and a positive attitude toward the possibilities that lie ahead.

Supportive feedback is your opportunity to reach out to your students with the caring attitude and reassurance that builds a solid relationship between teacher and students. Don't fall into the trap of taking students' appropriate behavior for granted. Let them know when you are proud of them and when they should feel proud of themselves.

The business world has long known the value of positively recognizing employees' efforts. Managers understand that positive recognition increases workers' motivation to perform well on the job, resulting in higher productivity and higher company-wide morale. Recognition such as "Employee of the Month," tangible rewards, and meaningful verbal praise are important corporate management techniques.

Supportive feedback is a powerful motivator for students of all ages. Consistently used, supportive feedback will:

➤ Encourage your students to continue appropriate behavior

➤ Increase your students' self-esteem

➤ Dramatically reduce problem behaviors

➤ Create a positive classroom environment for you and your students

➤ Help you teach behavior and establish positive relationships with your students

 Refer to *Assertive Discipline, 3rd Edition,* for an in-depth look at these benefits.

With these benefits in mind, let's take a look now at five ways you can provide supportive feedback to individual students:

1. Verbal recognition

2. Positive notes and phone calls home

3. Behavior awards and notes

4. Special privileges

5. Tangible rewards

Verbal Recognition

The most meaningful *and* effective means of supportive feedback you can give to secondary students are your own words of praise. Complimentary words from a caring teacher can positively effect a student long after the class ends and the student moves on.

It only takes a few seconds to say something positive about a student's responsible behavior or academic achievement. And this recognition says a great deal to a student:

> "I care about you. I notice the extra effort you're putting into your work. I'm proud of you and you should feel proud of yourself, too."

Verbal recognition should be your #1 choice when it comes to supporting your students' efforts in the classroom.

To make the recognition as effective as possible, keep these guidelines in mind:

Verbal recognition should be personal.

Middle schools and high schools—with their fast-paced schedules, bells, and busy hallways—can seem like a pretty impersonal place for freshmen and new students, as well as third- or fourth-year veterans. Let students know they are more than nameless faces in a crowd. Maximize the impact of your verbal recognition by including the student's name in your comments.

> "Maria, that was a great question you raised in class today. It made the discussion a lot more interesting for everyone."

Verbal recognition must be genuine.

Teenagers recognize sincere words when they hear them. Make sure what you say genuinely reflects your feeling of pride in a student's accomplishments. If your words ring false, they won't mean a thing.

Verbal recognition is descriptive and specific.

Verbal recognition will be most effective when it refers to something specific the student has accomplished. "I've noticed how well prepared for class you've been all this week, Sam, and your efforts are paying off in better grades!" sounds more meaningful than "Great job, Sam."

Secondary teachers often avoid supportive feedback and verbal recognition because they feel that older students simply cannot handle it. Some teachers are reluctant to give praise because students, uncomfortable with the recognition, may immediately revert to negative behavior. Others feel their praise is not valued because the student simply shrugs it off, ignores it, or makes a face that suggests extreme discomfort.

We thus are presented with a paradox: Adolescents are among the neediest of children for verbal recognition, support, and validation. Yet they make it the hardest for the adults in their lives to give to them. The need to be "cool," the need for peer acceptance, and the struggle to separate from parents and school often make adolescents overtly resistant to any attempt at positive reinforcement.

But in spite of the impression they give, secondary students *do* appreciate and want positive recognition. Your challenge as a teacher is to provide it skillfully and with care. It is up to you, therefore, to exercise professional judgment and sensitivity when openly recognizing a student. Some students will appreciate and enjoy a verbal and public "round of applause" from time to time. Other students will require a very private word of praise from you. Your goal is to build a student's self-esteem. With that in mind, deliver your comments in a manner that will be best received by the individual student.

The techniques within this section will help you develop a selection of supportive feedback ideas that will allow you to effectively reach and motivate most of your students. Applied with sensitivity and skill, these techniques will help you overcome the roadblocks that students may have in accepting recognition for their improvement and accomplishments.

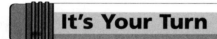

It's Your Turn

Start thinking now about all the opportunities you have each day to verbally recognize your students' successes—all the moments when an admiring word from you can make a big difference in a student's life. Jot notes in your plan book reminding yourself to look for students' positive behavior (or other achievement), then say something about it! Some teachers set a goal to give a minimum of five compliments per class period. Make that your goal, too, and you will be sure to positively reach at least 25–30 students each day.

Timely Reminders

As an extra reminder to consistently recognize students, make a copy of the "Time for Smart Choices" poster on page 17. Hang this reminder on the classroom wall right next to

the clock. Throughout the day, as you glance at the clock, this poster will be a reminder to keep looking for positive behavior—smart behavior choices—to reinforce.

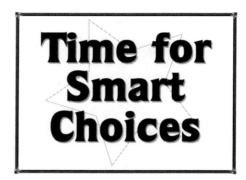

Looking for just the right moment to say "good for you"?

It is so easy to fall into the trap of being negative, yet there are hundreds of opportunities to recognize students each day of the year. Don't let these moments slip by. To help you further develop the habit, we've put together a list of 50 opportunities to say "You're terrific" (see page 18). Keep this sheet in your desk or plan book and review it from time to time as a reminder of all occasions throughout the school day in which you can verbally recognize a student's good behavior.

Time for Smart Choices

50 OPPORTUNITIES TO SAY "YOU'RE TERRIFIC"

RECOGNIZE STUDENTS FOR:

1 Arriving at class on time
2 Entering the classroom quietly
3 Cooperating while teacher takes attendance
4 Returning school forms on time
5 Transitioning into an activity
6 Following directions
7 Saying "please" and "thank you"
8 Listening attentively
9 Helping a classmate
10 Bringing necessary materials to class
11 Handing in homework
12 Being a polite audience at an assembly
13 Beginning work right away
14 Asking questions when unsure
15 Appropriate behavior during a test
16 Participating in a class discussion
17 Walking appropriately in the halls
18 Working cooperatively with a partner
19 Performing in a play or presentation
20 Putting away supplies and equipment
21 Good effort on an assignment
22 Assisting a new student
23 Sharing school experiences with parents
24 Making up missed assignments
25 Making a new friend

26 Good effort on a long-term project
27 Sharing
28 Being sensitive to others' feelings
29 Learning a new skill
30 Appropriate use of school property
31 Returning borrowed books and materials
32 Showing enthusiasm
33 Being responsible for a classroom job
34 Offering help without being asked
35 Not wasting paper and supplies
36 Staying on task
37 Telling the truth
38 Accepting a new challenge
39 Behaving when a guest is in the room
40 Reading at home
41 Participating in school functions
42 Demonstrating a positive attitude
43 Giving his/her best effort
44 Participating in a community improvement project
45 Participating in a group activity
46 Remaining calm during a problem situation
47 Showing creativity
48 Keeping busy when work is finished
49 Taking turns
50 Working cooperatively with an aide or volunteer

Positive Notes and Phone Calls Home

Usually, parents are notified only when there is a problem with their child at school. But how often do parents of secondary students hear *positive* news from teachers?

Don't underestimate the impact of positive communication between school and home. No matter how independent or aloof your students may appear, they still need encouragement and support. The goal of a positive note or phone call is to share with parents "good news" about their child. It is important for adolescents to know that you think enough of their successes to share them with their parents.

It's also a great way to establish a positive relationship with parents. Should a problem arise during the year, it will be much easier to gain that support when you need it if you have already begun building a positive foundation.

Finally, parents have enough to worry about when it comes to teenage sons and daughters. They will welcome and appreciate your encouraging comments about their child—comments that may be the first positive words they've heard about their child in years.

Positive phone calls and notes don't take much time, but they pay big dividends and need to be a part of your planning for supportive feedback.

Here's what a positive phone call to a parent might sound like:

> "Mr. Gibson? This is Ms. Wong, Todd's biology teacher. I just wanted to take a moment to let you know that Todd has made a terrific start in my class this year. We've spent a lot of time this first week going over lab procedures, and talking about the curriculum for the year. Todd has been enthusiastic in class and comes prepared every day. It looks like he's in for a terrific year.
>
> "Please tell Todd that I called and let him know how pleased I am to have him in my class."

Just that easy and just that quick. In a few brief moments, this teacher has established a positive relationship with a parent and boosted the self-esteem of a student.

And here's what a positive note might say:

> Dear Mr. and Mrs. Arias,
>
> Just a note to let you know what a great start Nicole is making in my English class. I can tell by the work she's turning in that she's working hard on her writing assignments. She has a real flair for expressing herself.
>
> Sincerely,
>
> *Ms. Wong*

It's Your Turn

Once you recognize how easy it really is to make positive contact with parents, you'll be convinced that it's an effective use of your time. The suggestions that follow will help you develop this positive parent involvement habit.

First, set goals!

If you're concerned that you have too many students to make positive parent communication a viable option, look at it this way: Set a goal to make a specific number of positive phone calls and to send a specific number of notes home each week. Just two contacts a day (10 a week) will guarantee that you reach 40 parents a month with good news. To make sure all students receive this important attention, keep track of your positive contacts by using the Positive Parent Communication Log on page 22. Scan or reproduce this form in your computer or make one copy for each class, and check off whenever good news goes home.

Once you break the ice with parents, particularly with good news, you may find yourself picking up the phone more often—just to pass along some friendly, encouraging words.

POSITIVE PARENT COMMUNICATION LOG

Use this sheet to keep track of your positive communication efforts by circling **N** for note, **PC** for phone call, and **O** for other.

Next, remember the good things that happen!

It's not always easy to remember the positive things students do during a busy day—especially when you have many students coming in and out of your classes. The answer? Use the Positive Memos on page 23 to jot down positive comments you want to remember and later share with parents in a note or phone call. Run off copies of the memos and keep a stack close at hand—different colors for different classes. During the day when something "memo"rable happens that you'd like to communicate, write it down! You may wish to keep this memo as part of a student's documentation file.

Finally, be sure to share the good news!

Use the reproducible positive notes on pages 24–29 any time you want parents and students to know how proud you are of student achievement. The "subject-specific" artwork on each note will let a parent know immediately who the note is from. Run off copies of these notes, keep them handy, and use them frequently! (Keep track of the notes you sent home by using the Positive Parent Communication Log on page 22.)

Fold-a-Note Cards

This is a perfect—and easy—way to send a message. Reproduce the Fold-a-Note Cards on page 30, cut along the dotted line, and you've got two note cards ready to use. Just write, staple shut, address, and mail.

At the beginning of the year, take a few minutes to have each student address at least one note. Collect and keep ready to use.

POSITIVE PARENT
COMMUNICATION LOG

Use this sheet to keep track of your positive communication efforts by circling **N** for note, **PC** for phone call, and **O** for other.

Student	Month of	Month of	Month of	Month of	Month of	Month of
	N PC O	N PC O	N PC O	N PC O	N PC O	N PC O
	N PC O	N PC O	N PC O	N PC O	N PC O	N PC O
	N PC O	N PC O	N PC O	N PC O	N PC O	N PC O
	N PC O	N PC O	N PC O	N PC O	N PC O	N PC O
	N PC O	N PC O	N PC O	N PC O	N PC O	N PC O
	N PC O	N PC O	N PC O	N PC O	N PC O	N PC O
	N PC O	N PC O	N PC O	N PC O	N PC O	N PC O
	N PC O	N PC O	N PC O	N PC O	N PC O	N PC O
	N PC O	N PC O	N PC O	N PC O	N PC O	N PC O
	N PC O	N PC O	N PC O	N PC O	N PC O	N PC O
	N PC O	N PC O	N PC O	N PC O	N PC O	N PC O
	N PC O	N PC O	N PC O	N PC O	N PC O	N PC O
	N PC O	N PC O	N PC O	N PC O	N PC O	N PC O
	N PC O	N PC O	N PC O	N PC O	N PC O	N PC O
	N PC O	N PC O	N PC O	N PC O	N PC O	N PC O
	N PC O	N PC O	N PC O	N PC O	N PC O	N PC O
	N PC O	N PC O	N PC O	N PC O	N PC O	N PC O
	N PC O	N PC O	N PC O	N PC O	N PC O	N PC O
	N PC O	N PC O	N PC O	N PC O	N PC O	N PC O
	N PC O	N PC O	N PC O	N PC O	N PC O	N PC O
	N PC O	N PC O	N PC O	N PC O	N PC O	N PC O
	N PC O	N PC O	N PC O	N PC O	N PC O	N PC O

POSITIVE MEMO

Student's name _____   Parent's name _____

Phone number _____   Date _____   Period/Class _____

Positive news to share with parents:

_____

_____

_____

_____

_____

© 2002 Solution Tree

POSITIVE MEMO

Student's name _____   Parent's name _____

Phone number _____   Date _____   Period/Class _____

Positive news to share with parents:

_____

_____

_____

_____

_____

© 2002 Solution Tree

POSITIVE MEMO

Student's name _____   Parent's name _____

Phone number _____   Date _____   Period/Class _____

Positive news to share with parents:

_____

_____

_____

_____

_____

© 2002 Solution Tree

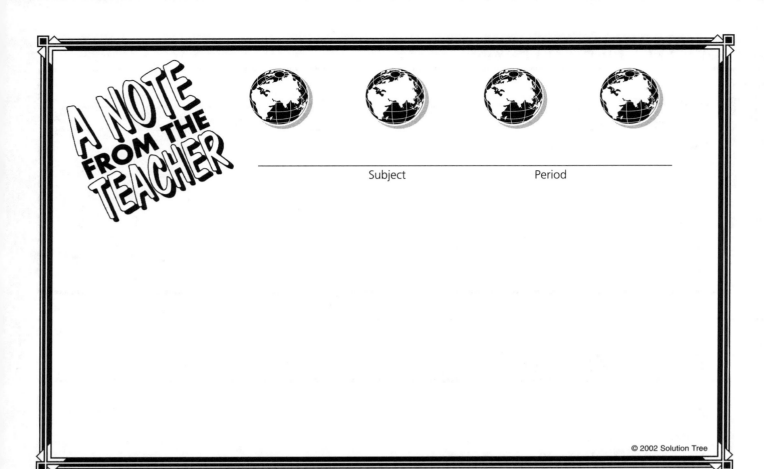

A NOTE FROM THE TEACHER

Subject   Period

© 2002 Solution Tree

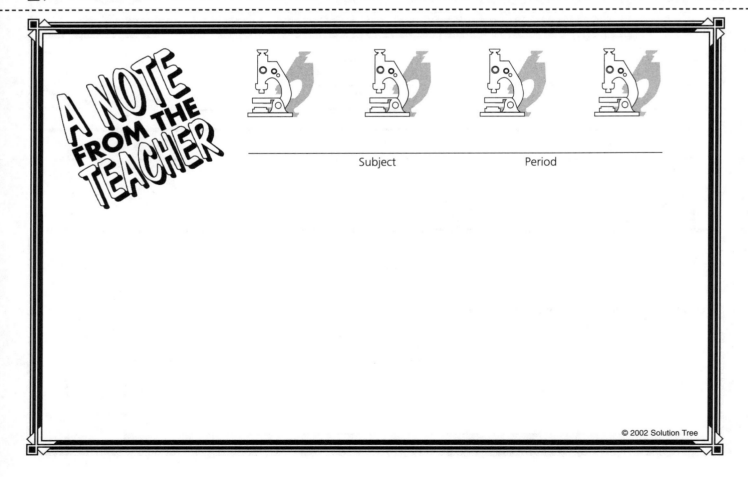

A NOTE FROM THE TEACHER

Subject   Period

© 2002 Solution Tree

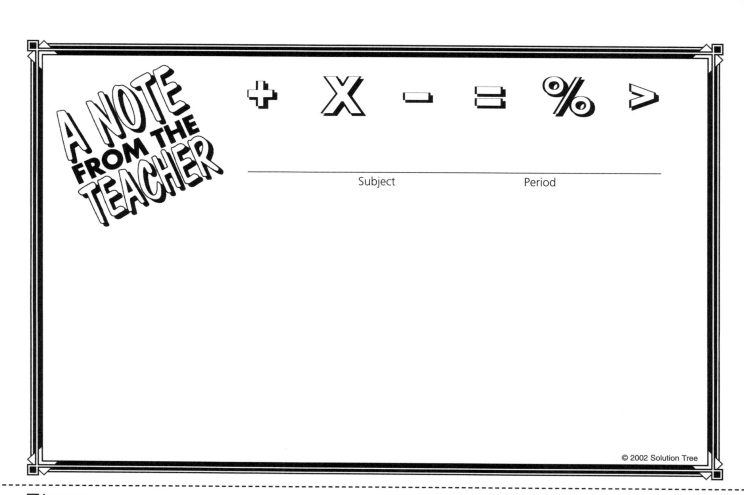

A NOTE FROM THE TEACHER

＋ X － ＝ ％ ＞

_____

Subject   Period

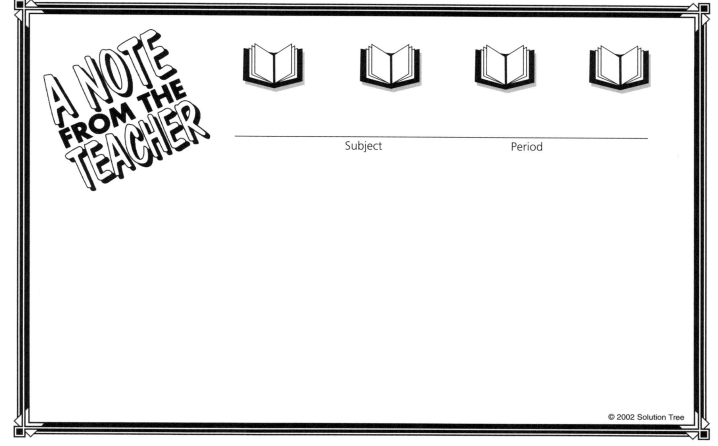

A NOTE FROM THE TEACHER

_____

Subject   Period

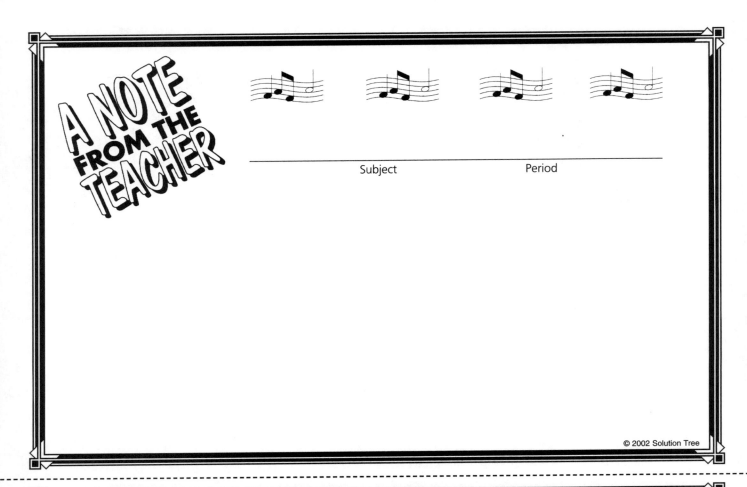

Subject   Period

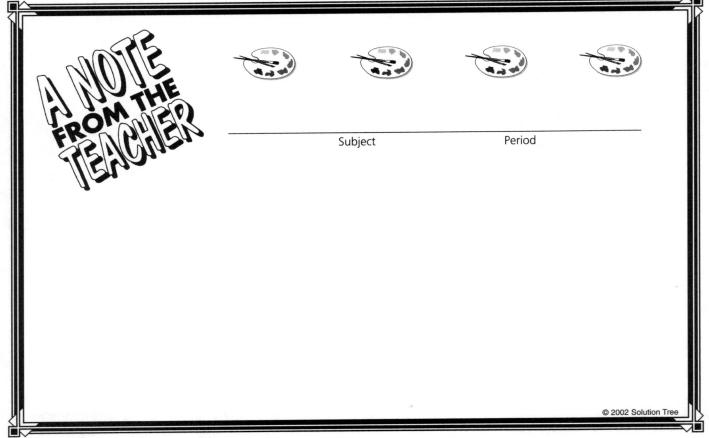

Subject   Period

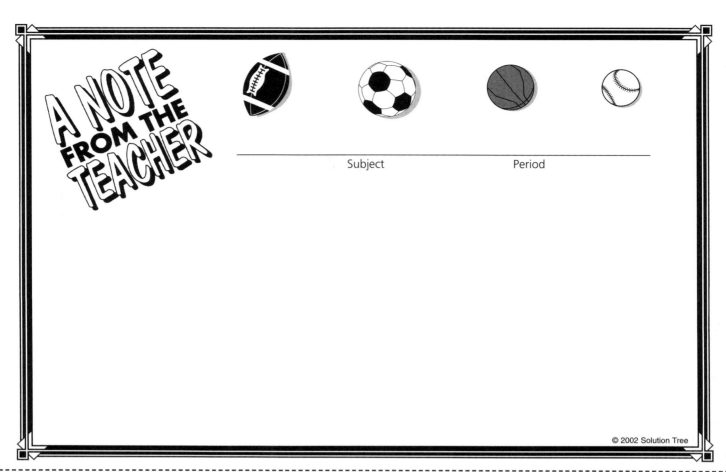

Subject _____ Period _____

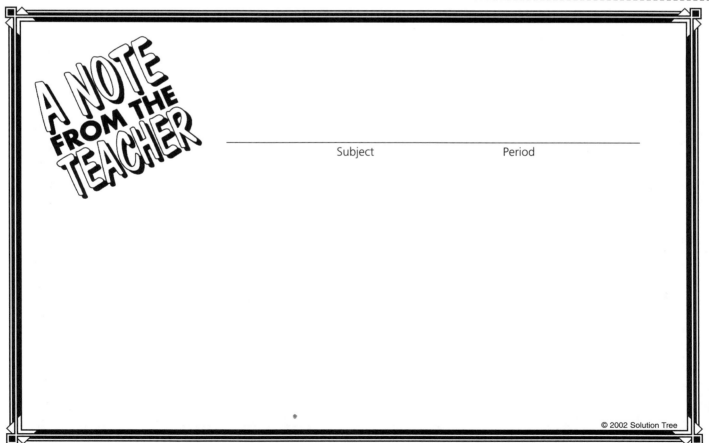

Subject _____ Period _____

Great News to Share!

_____

_____

_____

_____

_____
Signed   Date

GREAT! TERRIFIC! HOORAY! FABULOUS!

_____

_____

_____

_____

_____

_____

_____

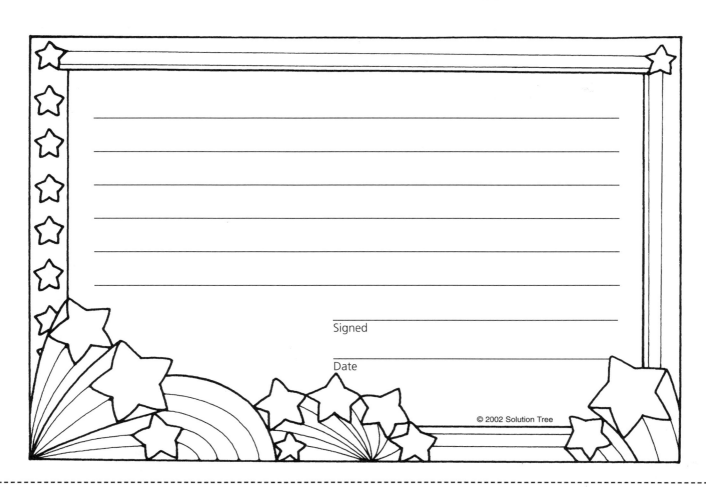

_____

_____

_____

_____

_____

_____

_____
Signed

_____
Date

© 2002 Solution Tree

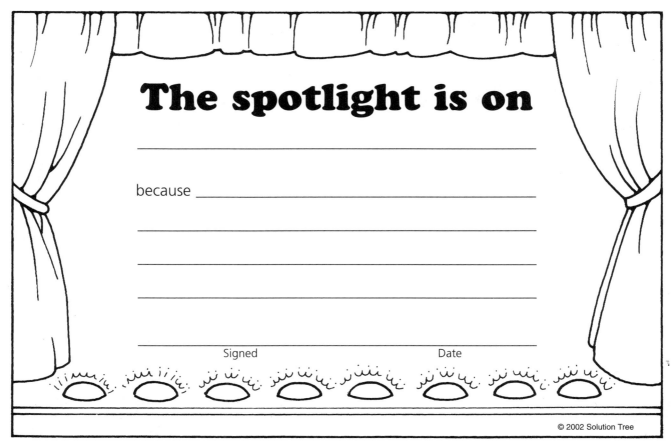

The spotlight is on

_____

because _____

_____

_____

_____

Signed   Date

© 2002 Solution Tree

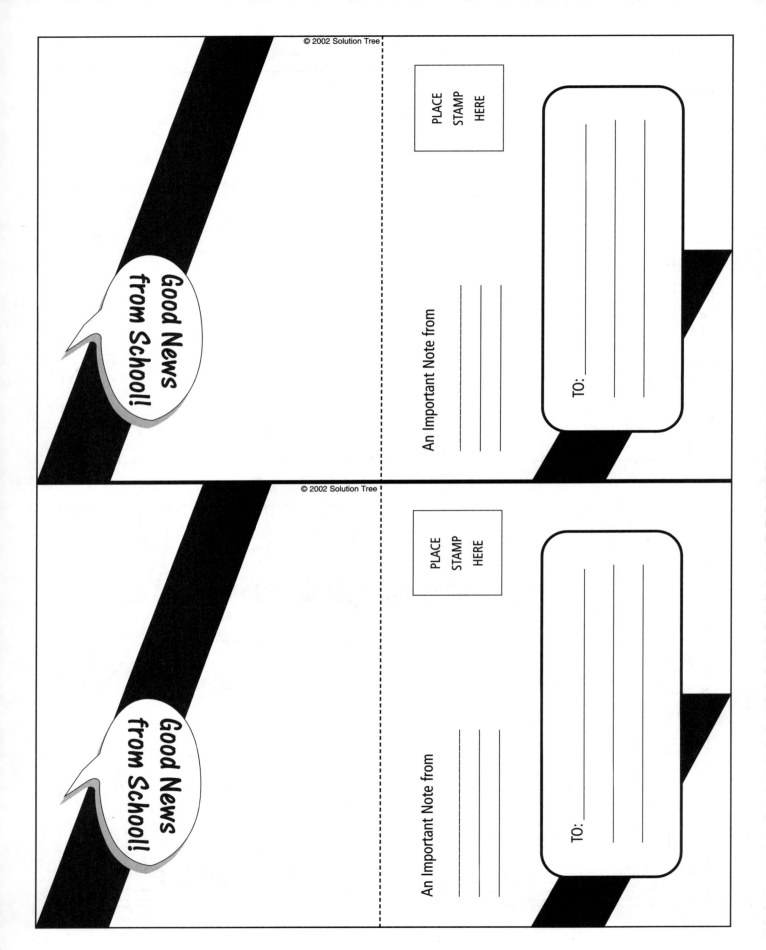

Behavior Awards and Notes

Recognition for a job well done is appreciated by students of any age. No matter how "cool" they appear to be, your students are no different from any of us when we are presented with tangible evidence that someone has noticed our good work.

They may stuff the "award" in a book with scarcely a glance, but chances are good that that piece of paper will later be taken out at home, read carefully, and perhaps even tucked away among the student's mementos.

The important thing to remember when giving a secondary student a tangible recognition is to take the time to add a personal note. A generic reproducible award with a hastily scrawled signature may not mean much, but a few lines of your own comments will mean a great deal.

Tell students that one way you'll recognize their responsible behavior throughout the year is by giving them special recognitions that let them *and* their parents know what a great job they are doing in school.

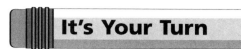

It's Your Turn

On the following pages, you will find a variety of items that can be used to recognize good behavior. They are designed especially for middle school and high school students.

Quick Notes to Parents

These Quick Notes are an easy way to send a speedy, positive message to parents. Keep a stack close by, and when you are grading papers and would like to share some positive news, just fill one out and staple to the paper. This is a great way to stay in touch with parents.

Quick Notes to Students

A teacher's written comments to a student can have a long-lasting and positive impact. Quick Notes are a simple way to pass along a few good words. Just fill them out and staple them to returned papers.

Clock Busters

Time is a precious commodity to an adolescent. That's why Clock Busters tickets will be well worth students' good behavior efforts. A Clock Buster ticket, earned for appropriate behavior, entitles a student to an extra day to turn in an assignment.

Here's how to use Clock Busters tickets:

Explain to students that when they receive a Clock Busters ticket, they are to save it to use sometime when they need an extra day to complete an assignment. (Clarify any expectations you may have, such as the due date for a long-term paper.) When they wish to redeem a ticket, students fill in a description of the assignment, fill in the due date, and sign the slip. To make record-keeping easy for you, draw a circle in your record book for the assignment due that day. The next day, the empty circle will remind you that the assignment from the day before is due.

Privilege Passes

Secondary students love getting out of class, even if it's only for a minute or two. Now they can earn the privilege by demonstrating exemplary classroom behavior. Students will gladly give their best efforts to earn the privilege of leaving class to get a drink, or go to the library, school bookstore, or restroom. When you want to reward a student, just fill in his or her name on a Privilege Pass and "pass" along a well-deserved award.

Good Behavior Bookmark/Raffle Ticket Combos

There's a bonus attached to these bookmarks! Each bookmark also contains a raffle ticket. Each time a student is awarded a bookmark, he or she also earns the right to enter a raffle drawing. The student fills the ticket out and deposits it into a class collection box. Once a week (or every two weeks, etc.) the teacher draws a predetermined number of tickets and awards privileges or prizes.

Or try this: At the beginning of the week, pass out a bookmark to every student. Explain that as the week goes by, you will recognize responsible behavior by allowing students to enter their ticket portion in a class raffle.

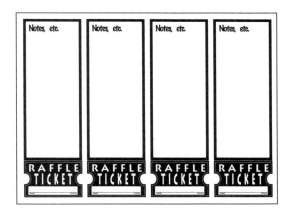

"Notables"

Just for students, these open-ended positive notes are designed to provide you with an appealing graphic background that will enhance your message and help you communicate your sincere words of appreciation.

Get the community involved!

Free items from local merchants are great positive rewards and motivators for students. This idea takes a little work up front, but the results are worth it, both in terms of motivating students *and* in generating community involvement.

Here's what to do:

1. Make copies of the School-Community Positive Recognition cards on page 44.

2. Notice that the cards contain space for student's name, name of school, and teacher's signature. The remaining spaces are blank.

3. Contact local merchants, asking them to become part of a positive recognition program for your classes. Explain that you want to give meaningful recognition to students who are making responsible behavior choices—and that as members of the community, the recognition they can offer is important.

   Ask each merchant to offer a "freebie" that the student receives when he or she brings a signed School-Community Positive Recognition Card into the place of business. Explain that students who are in possession of these cards will be those who have earned them through responsible behavior. (After a prize is redeemed, the merchant can "X" out the box or punch a hole through it.)

   Here are some examples of recognitions that merchants typically offer:

   Movie theater: Free box of popcorn

   Fast-food
   restaurant: Free hamburger

Convenience store:	Free soda or frozen drink
Skating rink:	Free pass or free skate rental
Bowling alley:	Free game or free shoe rental
Video store:	Free movie or video game rental
Ice-cream shop:	Free serving

4. Once you have collected enough recognitions, list them in the spaces on the card. Duplicate, cut out, and keep them available for use. Decide on parameters for use of the card (how a student can earn one) and introduce them to students.

5. Stay in contact with contributing merchants, and let them know how much you appreciate their involvement. Encourage students to say thanks, too.

Good Behavior "Designer" Bookmarks

Fun and functional, each of these bookmarks carries a positive message of recognition PLUS a graphic design that students can color in and keep. They are geared for early teens.

Behavior Certificates

Younger students and their parents will appreciate the humorous (but sincere) behavior certificates on pages 46–47. Just fill in the specific behavior you want to recognize and present it to the deserving student, or send it home to parents.

Certificate of Appreciation

The full-page certificate on page 48 can be used to recognize good behavior, or any other occasion deserving of praise.

QUICK NOTE
to Parents

To: _____

Just a note to let you know that

_____

_____

_____

_____

_____

_____
Signed   Date

© 2002 Solution Tree

QUICK NOTE
to Parents

To: _____

Just a note to let you know that

_____

_____

_____

_____

_____

_____
Signed   Date

© 2002 Solution Tree

QUICK NOTE
to Parents

To: _____

Just a note to let you know that

_____

_____

_____

_____

_____

_____
Signed   Date

© 2002 Solution Tree

QUICK NOTE
to Parents

To: _____

Just a note to let you know that

_____

_____

_____

_____

_____

_____
Signed   Date

© 2002 Solution Tree

QUICK NOTE
to Students

To: _____

Just a quick note to let
you know _____

_____

_____

_____

_____

_____
Signed   Date

© 2002 Solution Tree

QUICK NOTE
to Students

To: _____

Just a quick note to let
you know _____

_____

_____

_____

_____

_____
Signed   Date

© 2002 Solution Tree

QUICK NOTE
to Students

To: _____

Just a quick note to let
you know _____

_____

_____

_____

_____

_____
Signed   Date

© 2002 Solution Tree

QUICK NOTE
to Students

To: _____

Just a quick note to let
you know _____

_____

_____

_____

_____

_____
Signed   Date

© 2002 Solution Tree

Clock Busters!

You have earned the privilege of turning in an assignment one day after it's due!

To redeem, fill in this information:

Class/Period _____

Assignment _____

Due Date _____

Your Signature _____

Teacher's Signature _____

*Turn in this coupon on date assignment is due.

© 2002 Solution Tree

Clock Busters!

You have earned the privilege of turning in an assignment one day after it's due!

To redeem, fill in this information:

Class/Period _____

Assignment _____

Due Date _____

Your Signature _____

Teacher's Signature _____

*Turn in this coupon on date assignment is due.

© 2002 Solution Tree

Clock Busters!

You have earned the privilege of turning in an assignment one day after it's due!

To redeem, fill in this information:

Class/Period _____

Assignment _____

Due Date _____

Your Signature _____

Teacher's Signature _____

*Turn in this coupon on date assignment is due.

© 2002 Solution Tree

Clock Busters!

You have earned the privilege of turning in an assignment one day after it's due!

To redeem, fill in this information:

Class/Period _____

Assignment _____

Due Date _____

Your Signature _____

Teacher's Signature _____

*Turn in this coupon on date assignment is due.

© 2002 Solution Tree

Clock Busters!

You have earned the privilege of turning in an assignment one day after it's due!

To redeem, fill in this information:

Class/Period _____

Assignment _____

Due Date _____

Your Signature _____

Teacher's Signature _____

*Turn in this coupon on date assignment is due.

© 2002 Solution Tree

Clock Busters!

You have earned the privilege of turning in an assignment one day after it's due!

To redeem, fill in this information:

Class/Period _____

Assignment _____

Due Date _____

Your Signature _____

Teacher's Signature _____

*Turn in this coupon on date assignment is due.

© 2002 Solution Tree

Clock Busters!

You have earned the privilege of turning in an assignment one day after it's due!

To redeem, fill in this information:

Class/Period _____

Assignment _____

Due Date _____

Your Signature _____

Teacher's Signature _____

*Turn in this coupon on date assignment is due.

© 2002 Solution Tree

Clock Busters!

You have earned the privilege of turning in an assignment one day after it's due!

To redeem, fill in this information:

Class/Period _____

Assignment _____

Due Date _____

Your Signature _____

Teacher's Signature _____

*Turn in this coupon on date assignment is due.

© 2002 Solution Tree

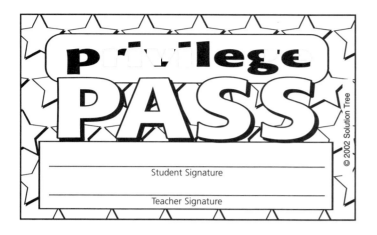

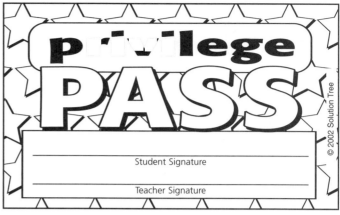

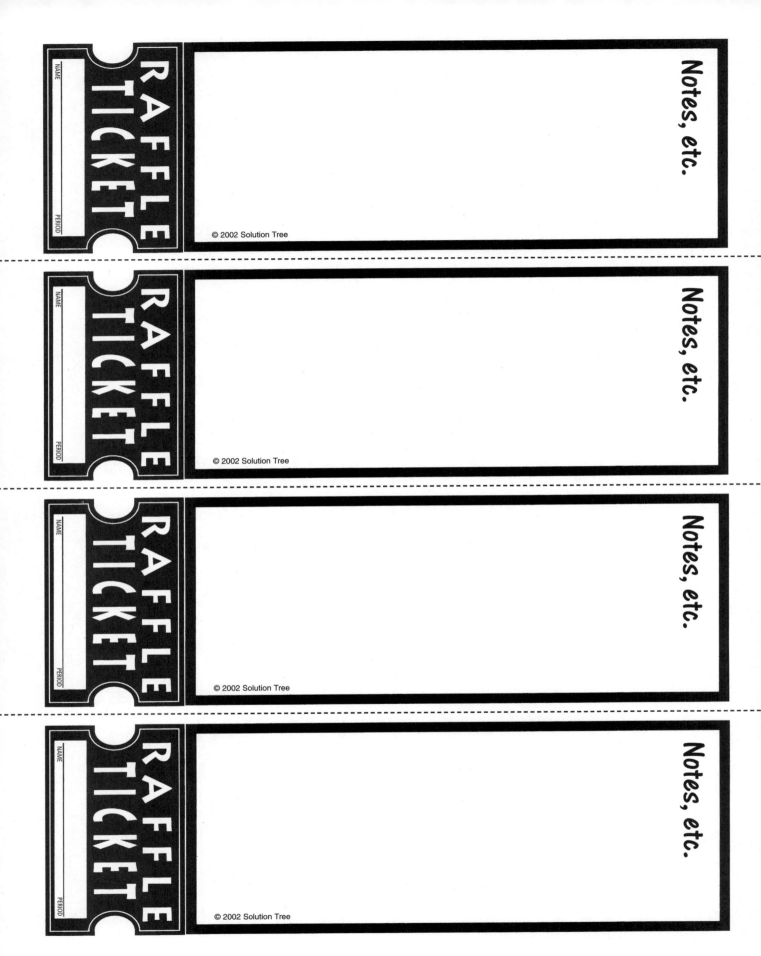

RAFFLE TICKET

NAME

PERIOD

Notes, etc.

© 2002 Solution Tree

RAFFLE TICKET

NAME

PERIOD

Notes, etc.

© 2002 Solution Tree

RAFFLE TICKET

NAME

PERIOD

Notes, etc.

© 2002 Solution Tree

RAFFLE TICKET

NAME

PERIOD

Notes, etc.

© 2002 Solution Tree

Razzle-Dazzle Raffle Ticket

NAME

Really Radical Raffle ticket

NAME

GREAT IMPRESSIONS RAFFLE TICKET

NAME

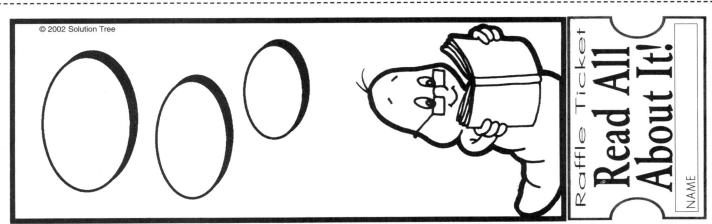

Raffle Ticket Read All About It!

NAME

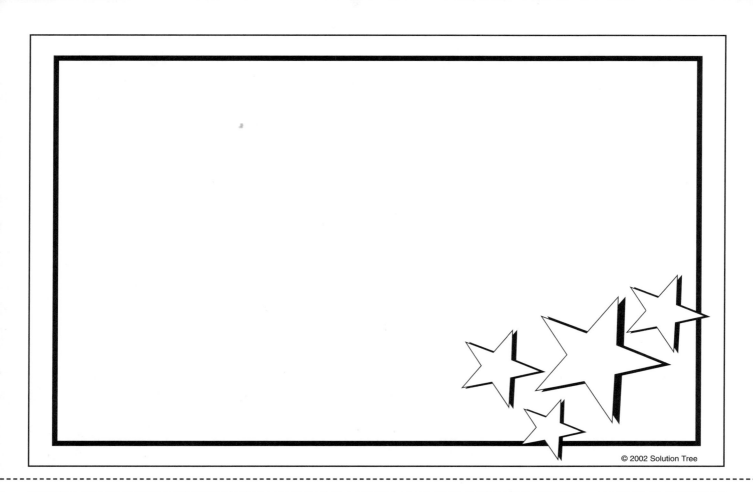

School-Community Positive Recognition

Student's name

School

Teacher's signature

© 2002 Solution Tree

School-Community Positive Recognition

Student's name

School

Teacher's signature

© 2002 Solution Tree

School-Community Positive Recognition

Student's name

School

Teacher's signature

© 2002 Solution Tree

School-Community Positive Recognition

Student's name

School

Teacher's signature

© 2002 Solution Tree

It's no puzzle . . .
Your behavior
is really together!

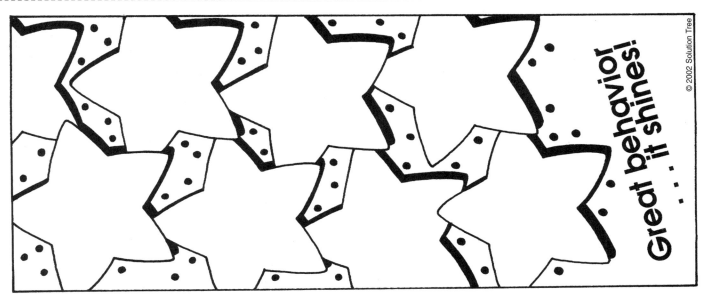

Great behavior!
. . . it shines!

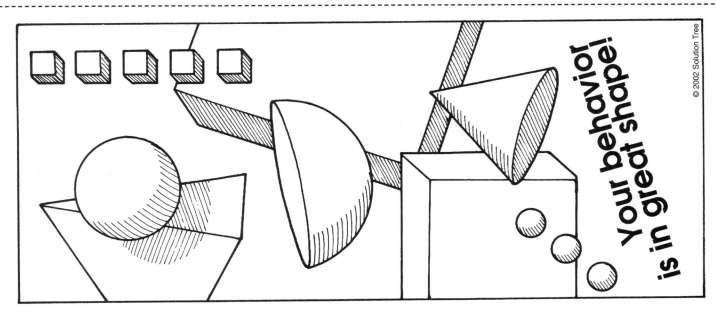

Your behavior!
is in great shape!

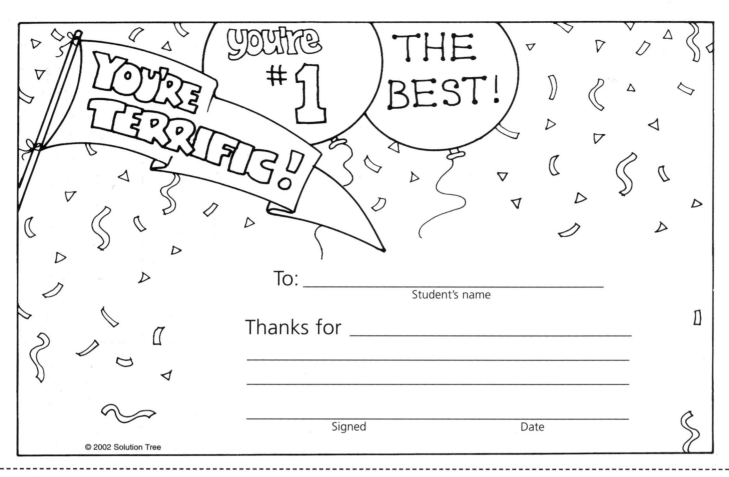

You're TERRIFIC!

you're #1

THE BEST!

To: _____
Student's name

Thanks for _____

_____

_____

_____
Signed   Date

© 2002 Solution Tree

School's a smooth ride when you behave like _____.
Student's name

SUPER

© 2002 Solution Tree

_____
Signed   Date

To: _____
Student's name

I'd like to say a few words about the way you behave in class . . .

_____
Signed   Date

To: _____
Student's name

Your responsible behavior has made you a star!

Thanks!

_____
Signed   Date

Certificate of

Appreciation

presented to

For

Teacher's Signature

Date

© 2002 Solution Tree

Special Privileges

When you want to recognize positive student behavior, and motivate your students to continue that behavior, allow them to take part in activities that they particularly enjoy.

Special privileges are great motivators because students like to receive them and they don't have to cost anything to give.

Here are some ideas to get you started. On the lines that follow, add ideas of your own that will appeal to your students.

➤ First excused after class

➤ Choose any seat in class for a day, a week, etc.

➤ Listen to music on cassette with headset

➤ 10 minutes of free time

➤ Extra computer time

➤ Work on favorite activity

➤ May leave room to get a drink

➤ _____

➤ _____

➤ _____

➤ _____

➤ _____

➤ _____

➤ _____

➤ _____

➤ _____

➤ _____

➤ _____

➤ _____

It's Your Turn

Just ask 'em!

Not sure what special privileges will motivate your students? They will be more than happy to give their opinions on this matter! Give students the Wish List menu on the next page. Before you reproduce the list, write some privileges that you would be comfortable offering to your students. After distributing, ask students to write in appropriate suggestions of their own.

Tell students that you want their feedback because throughout the year, you will be awarding special privileges to students who exhibit responsible behavior at school. Tie this activity into a brief class discussion, and you're sure to gather lots of motivating suggestions!

You earned it!

When a student earns a special privilege for responsible behavior choices, fill out a You Earned It! coupon. These open-ended coupons give students the good news and give you an easy way to present positive recognition. Add some praise of your own when you hand out the coupons and make the recognition even more meaningful.

"Filipina, you worked with your lab partner today without any disagreements or problems. Because of that, you completed your experiment on time. Here's a coupon worth an extra five points on Friday's quiz. You earned it!"

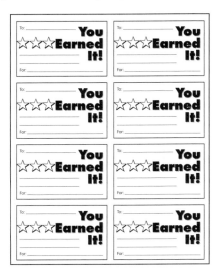

Get parents involved, too!

Send home a small supply of You Earned It! coupons to parents. In a brief note, encourage them to use the coupons at home to congratulate their children for good schoolwork, responsible behavior at school or at home, or as a recognition for being a caring member of the family. (Back-to-School Night is a good time to explain these coupons to parents and distribute copies to them.)

WISH LIST OF SPECIAL PRIVILEGES

Name _____ Class/Period _____

Check off three things that you like to do best in class. If you have any suggestions of your own, add them to the list.

❑ _____   ❑ _____
❑ _____   ❑ _____
❑ _____   ❑ _____
❑ _____   ❑ _____
❑ _____   ❑ _____

© 2002 Solution Tree

WISH LIST OF SPECIAL PRIVILEGES

Name _____ Class/Period _____

Check off three things that you like to do best in class. If you have any suggestions of your own, add them to the list.

❑ _____   ❑ _____
❑ _____   ❑ _____
❑ _____   ❑ _____
❑ _____   ❑ _____
❑ _____   ❑ _____

© 2002 Solution Tree

WISH LIST OF SPECIAL PRIVILEGES

Name _____ Class/Period _____

Check off three things that you like to do best in class. If you have any suggestions of your own, add them to the list.

❑ _____   ❑ _____
❑ _____   ❑ _____
❑ _____   ❑ _____
❑ _____   ❑ _____
❑ _____   ❑ _____

© 2002 Solution Tree

To: _____

For: _____

To: _____

For: _____

To: _____

For: _____

To: _____

For: _____

To: _____

For: _____

To: _____

For: _____

To: _____

For: _____

To: _____

For: _____

Tangible Rewards

Most students are motivated by verbal recognition, positive notes, and special privileges. You may, however, have one or two students who simply do not respond to these positive reinforcers. There are times when tangible rewards such as small prizes are the only positives that will work—the only motivation a student will respond to. When needed, use tangible rewards, but use them with care.

Follow these guidelines:

➤ Be sure to give a tangible reward immediately after you have observed the desired behavior. You want the student to associate this behavior with the reward.

➤ Whenever you give a student a tangible reward, always pair it with your own verbal recognition, such as:

> "Bill, here's a discount ticket for a cheeseburger and fries. It's yours for sitting quietly and paying attention during the lesson today. I really appreciate your cooperation."

> "Denise, here are two mints—one for you and one for a friend—my way of saying thanks for taking your seat so quickly and quietly when you came into the classroom today. We were all able to get to work right away."

➤ Use tangible rewards sparingly, or they will lose their effectiveness.

Tangible rewards are particularly effective on those hard-to-motivate days when students tend to become overly excited; for example, on Fridays, days before holidays, and when special school events are scheduled.

It's Your Turn

We've looked at five ways you can positively support students for following the rules of the classroom:

1. Verbal recognition

2. Positive notes and phone calls home

3. Behavior awards and notes

4. Special privileges

5. Tangible rewards

Now it's time to choose the supportive feedback you will use with individual students in your own classroom. Be sure to include positives that you are comfortable giving and, most importantly, ones that you will be able to give frequently and consistently.

When you're finished planning, enlarge the Supportive Feedback Poster on page 54 and write the activities you will use to support students' appropriate behavior. (Tuck the finished poster away with your supplies. You'll be using it when you introduce your classroom discipline plan to your students.)

SUPPORTIVE
★★★ *Feedback* ★★★ ★

Classwide Positive Recognition

Just as you recognize individual students for their appropriate behavior, you can also recognize your entire class for meeting expectations. A classwide positive recognition system is an effective way of motivating students to behave and is easy to use.

What is a classwide positive recognition system?

A classwide positive recognition system is a program in which all your students, not just one student, work together toward a positive reward that will be given to the entire class.

The goal of a classwide recognition system is to motivate students to learn new behavior or work on improving a problem behavior. It shows students how important it is to achieve a common goal. A classwide recognition system is especially effective at the beginning of the school year, when your goal is to create a cooperative, interdependent classroom community. You can also use a classwide recognition system during difficult months, such as December and June, when student behavior may be sliding.

Keep these points in mind when considering a classwide recognition system:

➤ A powerful reason why a classwide recognition system works well with older students is that it makes use of peer pressure. It's not uncommon for students to cooperatively remind each other, "Get in your seat! We only need four more points to get radio time on Friday."

➤ A classwide recognition system is particularly effective when working on a specific classwide problem behavior, such as students noisily entering the classroom.

➤ A classwide recognition system is also effective at the beginning of the year in classes such as PE, art, and science (labs), where students need to learn important procedures (getting and setting up equipment, cleaning up).

➤ To be effective, a classwide recognition system should be implemented only as needed throughout the year. It is not meant to be in effect at all times. A classwide recognition system is designed to be used as a prescription for correcting a specific problem.

Here's how to set up a classwide recognition program:

1. Pick a system that you are comfortable with and that is appropriate to the age of your students. (On pages 57–59, you will find directions and artwork for creating your own positive behavior bulletin board.)

2. Choose a classwide reward that you are comfortable giving, but make sure that whatever reward the class earns, it is something they will want to work toward.

   Here are some ideas for classwide rewards:

   ➤ Special movie or video with popcorn

   ➤ Class game: Who Wants to Be a Millionaire, Wheel of Fortune, Trivial Pursuit, Jeopardy! (These games can be educationally oriented, too—serving as a review.)

- ➤ Listen to music in class

- ➤ Class time to do homework

- ➤ Invite a special visitor to class

- ➤ Students bring snacks to share in class

3. Make sure students are able to earn the reward in a timely manner. Set a goal for how quickly you want the class to earn a reward. Then monitor the frequency with which you are awarding points to ensure that you and the students are on track. Secondary students should typically be able to earn the classwide reward in one to two weeks.

4. Be sure your program complies with school and district policies.

5. Once the class has earned points toward a classwide reward, do not take away points for misbehavior. In addition, all students, regardless of corrective actions that may have been necessary, must participate in the classwide reward. If you have to correct a student's behavior and then also take away the classwide reward, you are providing two corrective actions for one misbehavior.

Building Positive Relationships

Your supportive feedback—for both individual students and the entire class—will be greatly enhanced by the strength of your positive relationships with students. The adage "students don't care how much you know until they know how much you care" particularly applies to your behavior management efforts. Building relationships with students doesn't just happen. You need to plan ways to reach out and get to know all your students, even the most challenging ones.

Try some of the ideas that follow.

- ➤ Greet your students by name each morning as they enter your classroom.

- ➤ Look for opportunities throughout the day to chat with students about issues of importance to them besides classwork.

- ➤ Take a Student Interest Inventory at the beginning of the year to learn about your students' favorite activities (see page 60).

- ➤ Share appropriate personal information about yourself (your interests and experiences).

- ➤ Call a student after a bad day and discuss how the next day may be better.

- ➤ Call a student after a good day and compliment her success.

- ➤ Send get-well notes, or call home, if a student has been out sick for a while.

- ➤ Write positive notes to students and their parents.

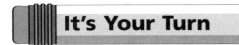
The following pages contain artwork and instructions for creating a positive behavior bulletin board, plus a Tell Me About You survey that you can reproduce and distribute to your students.

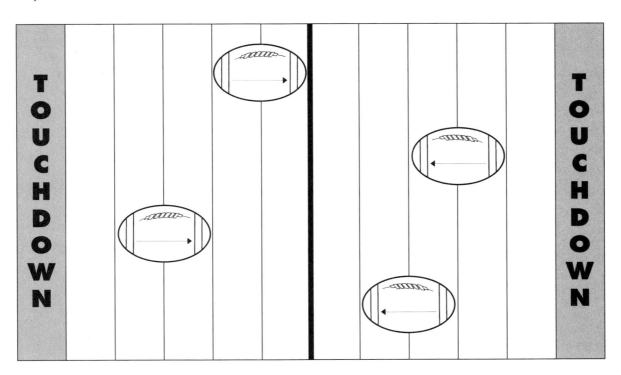

Touchdown!

Here's a classwide recognition system that will boost class spirit and encourage everyone to work together!

1. Cut out a football (pages 58–59) for every class that you want involved in this positive recognition "game."

2. To start, place footballs on the 20-yard line. The object is for each class, represented by a football, to advance forward and arrive at the opposite end zone before any of the other classes.

3. When students in a class meet predetermined behavioral goals, such as entering the classroom quietly or bringing all materials to class, the class earns the right to move forward to the next yard line. The first class to reach the end zone wins.

   Note: This classwide recognition system can also be used with an individual class not in competition with another.

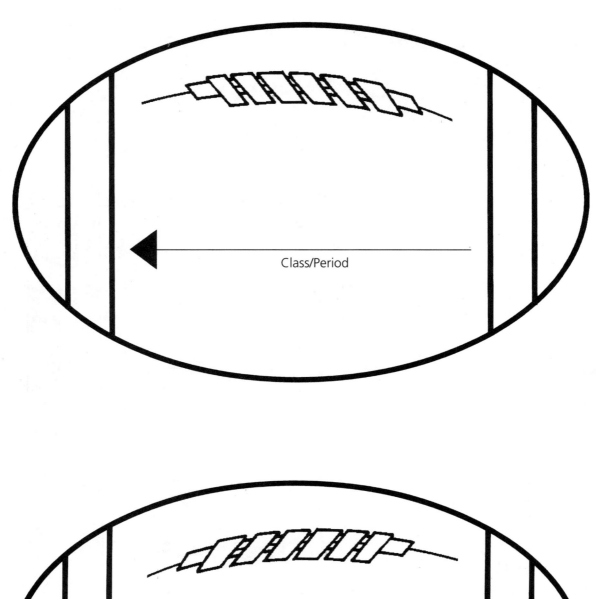

Class/Period

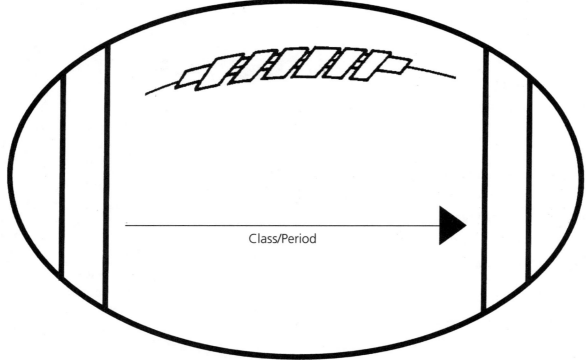

Class/Period

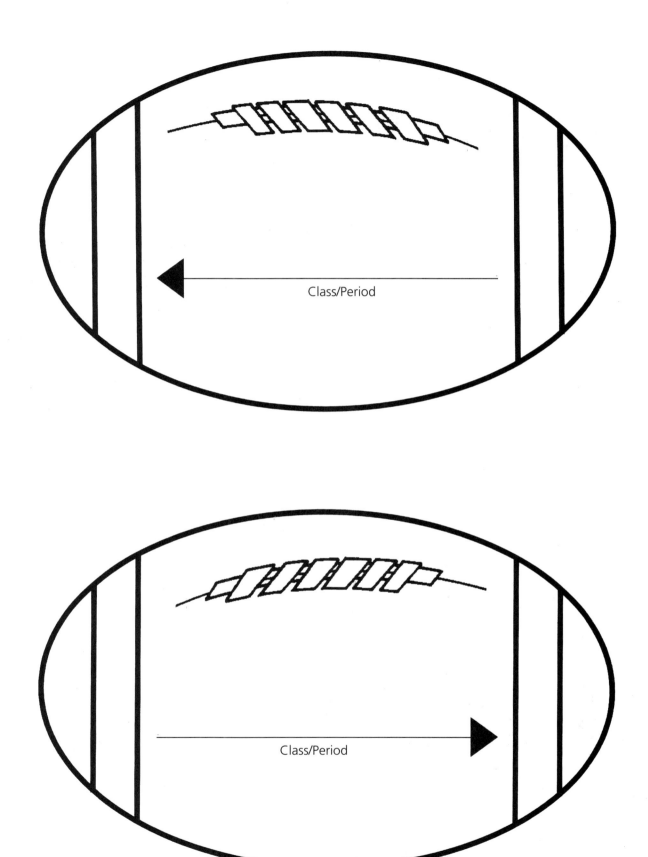

Class/Period

Class/Period

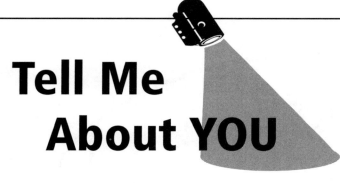

Tell Me About YOU

Welcome to my class! Getting to know you is important to me, and your answers to this survey will help. Your responses will be kept private, so please be honest. If you need more room to answer, use another sheet of paper or the back of this page.

Name: _____ Grade & Class: _____

Teacher: _____ Date: _____

Brothers and Sisters:

Name _____ Age _____

Name _____ Age _____

Name _____ Age _____

Name _____ Age _____

Special Friends: _____

_____

These are my favorite things to do: _____

_____

These are my favorites:

Book _____ Singer or group _____

Movie _____ Song _____

TV Show _____ Song _____

Some of the things that bug me are: _____

_____

I worry about: _____

_____

School would be better if: _____

_____

This is what a teacher did last year that I really liked: _____

_____

This is what a teacher did last year that bothered or upset me: _____

_____

One goal I'd like to accomplish this year: _____

_____

Creating Your Classroom Discipline Plan
Corrective Actions

In spite of the care you take in choosing your rules, and in spite of your consistent use of supportive feedback, there will be times when students will choose not to follow the rules of your classroom. When this disruptive behavior occurs, you must be prepared to deal with it calmly and quickly.

Corrective actions are the third part of your classroom discipline plan.

Why are corrective actions important?

By carefully planning in advance what you will do when students misbehave, you won't be caught off guard or left wondering how to respond to a student's misbehavior. And that means that students will be treated fairly and you will feel less stress.

Follow these guidelines when choosing corrective actions:

Corrective actions are fundamental for self-management.

Middle school and secondary school students are realizing that only they are responsible for their actions and their behavior. It's important, therefore, that students understand that if they *choose* to misbehave, certain actions will occur. When you give students a choice, you place responsibility where it belongs—with the student.

For example:

Teacher: Jordan, our classroom rule is "No yelling." If you break the rule again, you will choose to stay one minute after class. It's your choice.

Jordan: Okay. (*Within two minutes, Jordan yells to a friend across the room.*)

Teacher: Jordan, you're yelling again. You have chosen to stay one minute after class.

Remember: **Choice** is the key word. When you give students a choice, they learn that they can be in control of what happens to them. Keep in mind that corrective actions are not punishment. They are actions students know will occur should they choose to break the rules of the classroom. Corrective actions must be seen as natural outcomes of inappropriate behavior.

Corrective actions do not have to be severe to be effective.

Teachers often think that the more severe the corrective action, the more impact it will have on a student. This is not true. The key to their effectiveness is that they are used consistently. It is the inevitability of the corrective action that makes it effective. Minimal actions, such as remaining in the classroom one minute after the dismissal bell, can be as effective as after-school detention when they are given consistently.

Corrective actions must be things that students do not like, but they must never be physically or psychologically harmful.

How to Use Corrective Actions:
Establishing a Discipline Hierarchy

The best way to use corrective actions is to organize them into a discipline hierarchy as part of your classroom discipline plan. When placed in a hierarchy, corrective actions guide students toward self-management.

➤ The hierarchy is progressive, starting with a verbal reminder.

➤ The corrective actions then become gradually more substantial for the second, third, fourth, and fifth time that a student chooses to disrupt within a day.

Here's how the discipline hierarchy works:

First Time a Student Disrupts

Give a reminder the first time a student disrupts or breaks a classroom rule.

A reminder is important because it gives the student an opportunity to choose more appropriate behavior before a more substantial corrective action occurs.

Second or Third Time a Student Disrupts

The second or third time a student disrupts in the same period, you need to provide a corrective action.

These actions should be easy to implement and not time consuming. Typical corrective actions for second and third infractions include staying one or two minutes after class and writing in a behavior journal.

Fourth Time a Student Disrupts

Four disruptions during a class period are not acceptable. You need to contact parents if a student disrupts a fourth time in a period.

For some students, involving parents will be the only way you will motivate them to behave appropriately. Students need to know that you will be consistent in the enforcement of this corrective action.

Fifth Time a Student Disrupts

Sending a student to the principal, vice principal, counselor, or dean should be the last corrective action on your discipline hierarchy.

In preparation for implementing this corrective action, you must have already met with the administrator and discussed actions he or she will take when students are sent to the office.

Severe Clause

Sometimes you have to act quickly and decisively to stop a student's disruptive behavior. In the case of severe misbehavior, such as fighting, vandalism, defying a teacher, or in some way stopping the entire class from functioning, a student will not receive a warning. He or she loses the right to proceed through the hierarchy. Severe misbehavior calls for immediate removal of the student from the classroom.

At the top of the next page is a sample discipline hierarchy for secondary classrooms.

Refer to *Assertive Discipline, 3rd Edition,* for an in-depth look at using corrective actions.

Keeping Track of Corrective Actions

For your discipline hierarchy to be simple to use and easy to integrate into your teaching routine, you will need a system to keep track of student misbehavior and corrective actions accrued. You'll need to know at a glance the names of students who have received corrective actions, and where they are on the hierarchy. Keeping track doesn't have to be time consuming and, most important, it doesn't have to interrupt your teaching.

One method of keeping track of consequences is the Behavior Tracking Sheet (page 65). Another is the "8 in 1" sheet (page 66).

Using a Behavior Tracking Sheet

Here's how a Behavior Tracking Sheet works:

Make copies of the Behavior Tracking Sheet on page 65. Keep a sheet attached to a clipboard and close by you throughout the day.

Follow the guidelines below.

First time a student breaks a rule:

Write down his or her name on the sheet and say, for example, "Julie, the rule is 'Do not interrupt when someone else is speaking.' This is a reminder."

➤ Circle the "Reminder" designation on the tracking sheet.

Second time a student breaks a rule:

Speak quietly and calmly to the student, saying, for example, "Julie, this is the second time you have broken a rule in this classroom today. You have chosen to stay in class one minute after the bell rings."

➤ Circle the "2" on the tracking sheet. The student has been informed that she is to stay in the classroom for one minute after the bell rings.

Third, fourth, or fifth time a student breaks a rule:

If a student breaks a rule a third, fourth, or fifth time during the class period, you must continue speaking quietly and calmly to the student, and continue recording the infractions on the tracking sheet. Make sure that the corrective actions are given according to your hierarchy. If your fourth action is "call parents," be sure that you make that phone call. The success of your discipline plan depends upon your consistency.

Note: For some students, you may wish to jot down the rule broken. Then, if you notice a pattern of behavior developing, you will have documentation to help you solve that problem.

Name	MONDAY	TUESDAY	WEDNESDAY	THURSDAY	FRIDAY
Manuel	Reminder ② 3 4 5	Reminder 2 3 4 5	Reminder 2 3 4 5	Reminder 2 3 4 5	Reminder 2 3 4 5
	Reminder 2 3 4 5	Reminder 2 3 4 5	Reminder 2 3 4 5	Reminder 2 3 4 5	Reminder 2 3 4 5
	Reminder 2 3 4 5	Reminder 2 3 4 5	Reminder 2 3 4 5	Reminder 2 3 4 5	Reminder 2 3 4 5
	Reminder 2 3 4 5	Reminder 2 3 4 5	Reminder 2 3 4 5	Reminder 2 3 4 5	Reminder 2 3 4 5
	Reminder 2 3 4 5	Reminder 2 3 4 5	Reminder 2 3 4 5	Reminder 2 3 4 5	Reminder 2 3 4 5
	Reminder 2 3 4 5	Reminder 2 3 4 5	Reminder 2 3 4 5	Reminder 2 3 4 5	Reminder 2 3 4 5
	Reminder 2 3 4 5	Reminder 2 3 4 5	Reminder 2 3 4 5	Reminder 2 3 4 5	Reminder 2 3 4 5
	Reminder 2 3 4 5	Reminder 2 3 4 5	Reminder 2 3 4 5	Reminder 2 3 4 5	Reminder 2 3 4 5
	Reminder 2 3 4 5	Reminder 2 3 4 5	Reminder 2 3 4 5	Reminder 2 3 4 5	Reminder 2 3 4 5
	Reminder 2 3 4 5	Reminder 2 3 4 5	Reminder 2 3 4 5	Reminder 2 3 4 5	Reminder 2 3 4 5
	Reminder 2 3 4 5	Reminder 2 3 4 5	Reminder 2 3 4 5	Reminder 2 3 4 5	Reminder 2 3 4 5
	Reminder 2 3 4 5	Reminder 2 3 4 5	Reminder 2 3 4 5	Reminder 2 3 4 5	Reminder 2 3 4 5
	Reminder 2 3 4 5	Reminder 2 3 4 5	Reminder 2 3 4 5	Reminder 2 3 4 5	Reminder 2 3 4 5
	Reminder 2 3 4 5	Reminder 2 3 4 5	Reminder 2 3 4 5	Reminder 2 3 4 5	Reminder 2 3 4 5
	Reminder 2 3 4 5	Reminder 2 3 4 5	Reminder 2 3 4 5	Reminder 2 3 4 5	Reminder 2 3 4 5

BEHAVIOR TRACKING SHEET WEEK OF _____

To the teacher: When a student receives a reminder, write the student's name on this tracking sheet. If a student breaks additional rules during the school day, circle each corrective action on the appropriate box. For example, if a student receives a reminder and chooses not to follow the rules again during the day, you would record Reminder ② ③ 4 5

BEHAVIOR TRACKING SHEET

WEEK OF _____

Name	MONDAY	TUESDAY	WEDNESDAY	THURSDAY	FRIDAY
	Reminder 2 3 4 5	Reminder 2 3 4 5	Reminder 2 3 4 5	Reminder 2 3 4 5	Reminder 2 3 4 5
	Reminder 2 3 4 5	Reminder 2 3 4 5	Reminder 2 3 4 5	Reminder 2 3 4 5	Reminder 2 3 4 5
	Reminder 2 3 4 5	Reminder 2 3 4 5	Reminder 2 3 4 5	Reminder 2 3 4 5	Reminder 2 3 4 5
	Reminder 2 3 4 5	Reminder 2 3 4 5	Reminder 2 3 4 5	Reminder 2 3 4 5	Reminder 2 3 4 5
	Reminder 2 3 4 5	Reminder 2 3 4 5	Reminder 2 3 4 5	Reminder 2 3 4 5	Reminder 2 3 4 5
	Reminder 2 3 4 5	Reminder 2 3 4 5	Reminder 2 3 4 5	Reminder 2 3 4 5	Reminder 2 3 4 5
	Reminder 2 3 4 5	Reminder 2 3 4 5	Reminder 2 3 4 5	Reminder 2 3 4 5	Reminder 2 3 4 5
	Reminder 2 3 4 5	Reminder 2 3 4 5	Reminder 2 3 4 5	Reminder 2 3 4 5	Reminder 2 3 4 5
	Reminder 2 3 4 5	Reminder 2 3 4 5	Reminder 2 3 4 5	Reminder 2 3 4 5	Reminder 2 3 4 5
	Reminder 2 3 4 5	Reminder 2 3 4 5	Reminder 2 3 4 5	Reminder 2 3 4 5	Reminder 2 3 4 5
	Reminder 2 3 4 5	Reminder 2 3 4 5	Reminder 2 3 4 5	Reminder 2 3 4 5	Reminder 2 3 4 5
	Reminder 2 3 4 5	Reminder 2 3 4 5	Reminder 2 3 4 5	Reminder 2 3 4 5	Reminder 2 3 4 5
	Reminder 2 3 4 5	Reminder 2 3 4 5	Reminder 2 3 4 5	Reminder 2 3 4 5	Reminder 2 3 4 5
	Reminder 2 3 4 5	Reminder 2 3 4 5	Reminder 2 3 4 5	Reminder 2 3 4 5	Reminder 2 3 4 5
	Reminder 2 3 4 5	Reminder 2 3 4 5	Reminder 2 3 4 5	Reminder 2 3 4 5	Reminder 2 3 4 5
	Reminder 2 3 4 5	Reminder 2 3 4 5	Reminder 2 3 4 5	Reminder 2 3 4 5	Reminder 2 3 4 5
	Reminder 2 3 4 5	Reminder 2 3 4 5	Reminder 2 3 4 5	Reminder 2 3 4 5	Reminder 2 3 4 5

To the teacher: When a student receives a reminder, write the student's name on this tracking sheet. If a student breaks additional rules during the school day, circle each corrective action on the appropriate box. For example, if a student receives a reminder and chooses not to follow the rules again during the day, you would record Reminder ②③ 4 5

Using an "8 in 1" Tracking Sheet

Here's an easy tracking method that fits right in your pocket!

➤ Fold a sheet of line paper into quarters as shown.

➤ Write the date on the top of the sheet.

➤ In each of the eight sections (front and back), designate a period:

Period 1, Period 2, Period 3, etc.

➤ During the period, if a student breaks a rule or disrupts, simply write his or her name following it with the number of the classroom rule broken. (If you use this method, your classroom rules must be numbered: For example, Rule #1— Follow directions.)

In the sample below, you can see that Jeff Z. has broken Rule #1. Later in the period he breaks Rule #3.

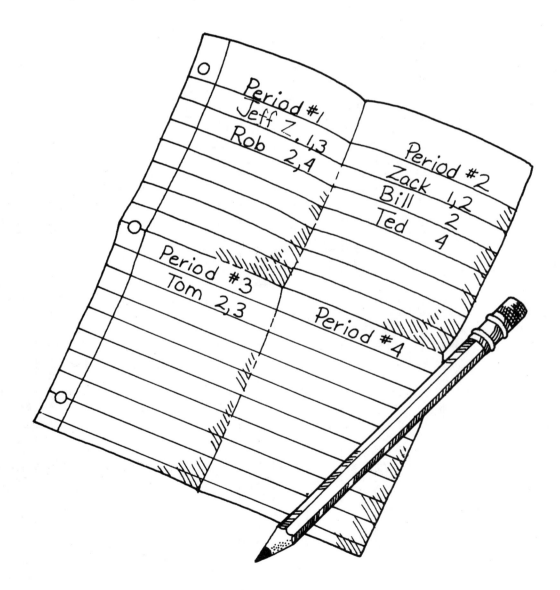

Suggested Corrective Actions

Here are some time-tested ideas that have been proven effective with secondary students:

One-Minute Wait After Class

It sounds deceptively simple, but this corrective action is very effective. You simply have the student wait one minute after the other students have been dismissed for recess, lunch, home, or the next period. One minute may not seem like a lot of time, but it can be an eternity to a student who wants to be first in line at the cafeteria, sit with a friend on the bus, hurry to his locker, or walk to the next class with her group.

A one-minute wait after class is an appropriate corrective action for the second time a rule is broken within a period. A two-minute wait is appropriate the third time a rule is broken.

> *Note:* If use of this corrective action (particularly a two-minute wait after class) is likely to cause a student to be late to his or her next class, you may wish to explain your plan to other staff members who may not want their students to be late. An alternative to a two-minute wait may be to have the student report back to class during lunch, recess, or before or after school to write in a Behavior Journal (see below).

Time Out—Removing a Student from the Group

Removing a disruptive student from the group is not a new concept, but it is a very effective corrective action for some students. Designate a desk or table as the "time-out" area, or simply relocate the student to a place in the room where she will not be likely to repeat the disruptive behavior. Depending upon the age of the student, a trip to the time-out area could last from 5 to 15 minutes.

> *Note:* It's very important that students not be isolated from the rest of the class for long lengths of time. Keep your time within these limits.

While separated from the rest of the class, the student continues to do his or her classwork.

Written Assignment in Behavior Journal

You want more from corrective actions than simply stopping a student's disruptive behavior. You also want the student to learn from the experience. That's critical if a student is to learn to become responsible for his own behavior. You want him to think about his behavior, and how he can choose to behave differently in the future.

When a student breaks a classroom rule, have her write a Behavior Journal account of her misbehavior. This can be done after class, during lunch break, during study hall, or at home. This written account should include the following points:

1. The rule that was broken

   The rule I broke was "No swearing in class."

2. Why the student chose to break the rule or not follow the direction

I swore at Arnie because he was putting me down. He was making me really mad.

3. What alternative action the student could have taken that would have been more appropriate

Instead of swearing at Arnie, I could have ignored him. I could have walked away and sat with my friends.

The student signs and dates the Behavior Journal sheet. The sheet should then be added to the student's documentation records. (It can also be sent home to parents as documentation of the student's misbehavior.)

Writing in a Behavior Journal helps students accept responsibility for their behavior. It also helps them think about choosing alternative behaviors in the future.

The Behavior Journal sheet can also be used as the focus for a meeting with the student to discuss how teacher and student can work together to improve the problem behavior. Writing in a Behavior Journal helps students accept responsibility for their behavior. It also helps them think about choosing alternative behaviors in the future.

Writing a Letter Home

Here's another corrective action that can prove effective with students:

The third time a student breaks a rule, she writes a brief letter home telling her parents about the rule that was broken. If the student breaks a rule a fourth time, the letter is mailed.

It's Your Turn

On page 69 you will find a reproducible Behavior Journal sheet. Make copies of this sheet and use it as part of your discipline hierarchy.

Write the corrective actions you choose on the poster on page 70.

BEHAVIOR JOURNAL

You have chosen to break a classroom rule. Please use this page to reflect on your own behavior. Remember, you are in control of what happens to you. You are responsible for your own actions.

Name: _____ Date: _____

THIS IS THE CLASSROOM RULE I CHOSE NOT TO FOLLOW:

THIS IS WHAT HAPPENED:

THIS IS WHY MY BEHAVIOR WAS NOT APPROPRIATE:

THIS IS WHAT I COULD HAVE DONE INSTEAD:

Student's signature:_____ Date: _____

CORRECTIVE ACTIONS

BEHAVIOR JOURNAL

You have chosen to break a classroom rule. Please use this page to reflect on your own behavior. Remember, you are in control of what happens to you. You are responsible for your own actions.

Name: _____ Date: _____

THIS IS THE CLASSROOM RULE I CHOSE NOT TO FOLLOW:

_____

_____

THIS IS WHAT HAPPENED:

_____

_____

_____

_____

THIS IS WHY MY BEHAVIOR WAS NOT APPROPRIATE:

_____

_____

_____

_____

_____

THIS IS WHAT I COULD HAVE DONE INSTEAD:

_____

_____

_____

_____

_____

Student's signature: _____Date: _____

CORRECTIVE ACTIONS

_____

_____

_____

_____

_____

_____

_____

_____

_____

_____

Launching Your Classroom Discipline Plan

Your discipline plan is written. You've chosen the rules for your classroom, the supportive feedback you will give when students follow the rules, and the corrective actions you will take when your students choose to break the rules.

Ready to put it all into action?

Not quite.

The success of your classroom discipline plan depends on more than your planning and involvement alone. It also depends on the informed involvement of the others who will be affected by it: your students, your students' parents, and your administrator.

In this section of the *Assertive Discipline Secondary Workbook*, we will look at techniques for introducing your discipline plan. Also included is a selection of reproducibles to help you plan and carry out an effective introduction.

Talk to Your Principal About Your Classroom Discipline Plan

No matter how well prepared you are, no matter how consistently and positively you use your discipline plan, you will still have some students that you will not be able to influence on your own. For these challenging students, you are going to need the cooperation and assistance of your principal, vice principal, dean, or counselor(s). It is best to involve him or her at the very beginning.

Before you put your classroom discipline plan into effect, you must meet with the appropriate administrator to discuss his or her role in your discipline plan.

This involvement is important for two reasons.

First, if you send a student to the office, according to the discipline hierarchy, the administrator will want to know what steps you have already taken.

Second, so that you can follow up with a student, you will want to know exactly what action will be taken when a student is sent to the office.

Make an appointment before school begins with the person responsible for dealing with discipline issues at your school. Follow these guidelines for presenting your plan:

Explain your rationale for using a classroom discipline plan.

Explain that you are committed to having a classroom that is safe and orderly—a positive learning environment for your students, and a positive teaching environment for yourself. Explain that this is the reason you have established a classroom discipline plan with rules for behavior, supportive feedback when students follow the rules, and actions that will correct the behavior of students who choose to break the rules.

Emphasize that you will attempt to handle behavior problems on your own before you ever ask for the principal's help.

Your principal (vice principal, dean, or counselor) needs to know that before you send a student to the office, you first will have taken steps to deal with the student on your own.

Ask for input.

Prepare a copy of your classroom discipline plan for the administrator. During your meeting, ask for input to make sure that he or she is comfortable with all aspects of the plan. If your administrator is not comfortable, ask for assistance in modifying the plan.

Discuss what will happen when a student is sent from your class to the office.

You need to know exactly what will happen when you send a student to the office.

Many administrators follow the hierarchy of consequences, such as:

First time sent to office:
Counsel with the student and suggest other ways the student could have handled the situation.

Second time sent to office:
Hold a parent conference to discuss the problem. Ask parents to support the school's efforts at home.

Third time sent to office:
In-school suspension. The student does schoolwork outside of the regular classroom and in a closely supervised environment.

Severe:
Counsel with the student and have a parent conference.

It is important for your administrator to let you know what type of disciplinary action will be taken so that you can follow up appropriately with the parents and the student. This can be accomplished by sending a note home or having a short meeting after school.

Discuss what will happen if the administrator is out of the building.

There may be times when you need to remove a disruptive student from your class and the principal or vice principal is not in the building. Clarify what you should do in this circumstance.

Here are two alternatives:

➤ Send the student to an alternative person.

➤ Send the student to "time out" in another classroom.

With prior consent of another teacher, a disruptive student is sent to a higher-grade classroom. When the student reaches the other classroom, he or she sits in a prearranged area away from the rest of the class. The student does not participate in the class activities and either sits quietly or does his or her own academic work.

Your administrator is an important part of your behavior management team. As such, the administrator needs to be informed in advance of his or her involvement and the support you expect. By introducing your discipline plan, you will assure your administrator that you are prepared to deal with student misbehavior on your own before asking for administrative assistance. And by mutually establishing what action your administrator will take, you will help ensure that discipline problems will be handled in a fair and consistent manner by both of you.

Teach Your Classroom Discipline Plan to Your Students

A list of rules posted on your classroom wall is not enough to motivate students to always follow those rules. You must actively involve your students in the plan.

Teaching your classroom discipline plan to your students is as important as any lesson you will teach during the year. This lesson should take place the first day of school—and it must take place in every class that you teach.

The lesson should cover the following points:

1. Explain why you need rules.

2. Teach the rules.

3. Check for understanding.

4. Explain how you will support students who follow the rules.

5. Explain why you need to use corrective actions when students do not follow the rules.

6. Explain the corrective actions.

7. Check for understanding.

Here are some suggestions for teaching your lesson:

1. Explain why you need rules.

Give a brief rationale for why you have rules in the classroom. Explain that you need to be able to teach, and students need to be able to learn. For both of these things to happen, everyone needs appropriate behavior in the classroom. Make a brief analogy to "on the job" rules, or traffic rules, that students have probably experienced by now. Point out that there are rules in the workplace so that the job can get done. There are traffic rules we must obey so people can safely get from one place to another. Likewise, there are classroom rules so that students can get their job done at school—safely and successfully.

2. Teach the rules.

Clearly explain each of your classroom rules. Very briefly talk about why each rule is necessary and why you have chosen it. For example, the rule "Be in your seat when the bell rings" is necessary to make sure that lessons begin on time. By beginning lessons on time, you will be able to cover the material your students need to be successful in school.

3. Check for understanding.

Take the time to make sure that all students understand the rules you've taught. Ask if there are any questions and make sure that students understand that these rules are in effect at all times—during all activities.

4. Explain how you will support students who follow the rules.

Supportive feedback is going to be the most important part of your classroom discipline plan. Tell your students again that you know they can all be successful at following the classroom rules, and that throughout the year you will recognize and reward those students who follow the rules. Pique student enthusiasm by detailing the supportive feedback system you will use. Increase interest further by asking students to suggest positive ideas that they'd like to see used.

> "See these You've Earned It! coupons? From time to time, I'll be giving these coupons to students who follow the rules and follow directions. I'll be filling in the coupons with special privileges you would like to earn."

Keep this in mind: The manner in which you present your discipline plan to your students will set the tone for your classroom for the entire year. Be positive. Communicate your high expectations. Emphasize to your students that you believe they will choose to follow the rules and enjoy the rewards of their positive behavior. However, students must also understand that if they choose to break a rule, you will take actions to help them correct their inappropriate behavior.

5. Explain why you need to use corrective actions when students do not follow the rules.

Explain to students that they are responsible for the behavioral choices they make. They need to know that when they choose to break a rule, they will also be choosing the corrective actions that follow. Explain that whenever one makes poor choices in life, there are often consequences to those choices. It's true in the workplace, it's true at home, and it's true in school.

> "What would happen if you showed up late for work?"

> "What would your boss do if you decided to behave inappropriately on the job?"

6. Explain the corrective actions.

Tell students what you will do if they choose to misbehave once in a class period (e.g., give a reminder), twice in a period, three times, four times, and five times in a period. Explain how you will keep track of their behavior.

> "See this clipboard? (*Hold it up.*) I'm going to keep it near me during the period. The first time you break a rule and disrupt the class, I will write your name on the clipboard. I'll also remind you of what the rules are. For example, if I hear a student swearing in class, all I will say to you is 'Juan, I want to remind you that the rule is "No swearing in the classroom." That's a reminder.'

> "That's all I'll do.

> "The reminder gives you a chance to choose more appropriate behavior. Use this signal wisely to change what you're doing.

> "But if you do break this rule again, or any other rule during the period, I'll circle 2 on the chart. This means that you've broken a rule two times, even if it's not the same rule, and this means that you have chosen to stay after class for one minute. I know one minute doesn't sound like a lot of time, but your friends will not be permitted to wait for you, and you will not be allowed to talk to anyone or move out of your seat until that minute is up. This will give you time to think about your behavior and plan to behave more appropriately the next time you come to class.

"The third time you break a rule, you will stay after class for two minutes and complete a Behavior Journal sheet, which you will take home and have signed by your parent *(optional).*" *(Give students a step-by-step explanation for completing the Behavior Journal sheet.)*

Go through the rest of your discipline hierarchy in this manner, explaining each step. Afterward, take the time to emphasize your belief that the students can behave—and can act responsibly.

"I know that all of you can follow our classroom rules. I know that all of you can make good decisions about how you speak, work, and interact with your classmates. By making responsible choices, you can make this your most successful and enjoyable year yet."

7. Check for understanding.
It's important that all students understand the corrective actions you will use in the classroom. Ask if they have any questions.

Keep this in mind: The manner in which you present your discipline plan to your students will set the tone for your classroom for the entire year. Be positive! Communicate your high expectations. Emphasize to your students that they will all choose to follow the rules and enjoy the rewards of their good behavior. However, students must also understand that you will take action to correct their behavior if they choose to break a rule.

> Refer to *Assertive Discipline, 3rd Edition,* for additional sample scripts for teaching this lesson.

It's Your Turn

Teaching your classroom discipline plan is an important lesson, one that will impact your classroom environment for the rest of the year. Take the time to carefully plan the lesson. Use the Lesson-Planning Worksheet on pages 77 and 78 as you organize your lesson.

TEACHING YOUR
CLASSROOM DISCIPLINE PLAN
LESSON-PLANNING WORKSHEET

Use this worksheet to create your classroom discipline plan.

1. Explain why you need rules.

_____

_____

_____

_____

2. Teach the rules.

_____

_____

_____

_____

3. Check for understanding.

_____

_____

_____

_____

4. Explain how you will support students who follow the rules.

_____

_____

_____

_____

5. Explain why you need to use corrective actions.

_____

_____

_____

_____

_____

_____

_____

6. Explain the corrective actions.

_____

_____

_____

_____

_____

_____

_____

7. Check for understanding.

_____

_____

_____

_____

_____

_____

_____

After you've taught the lesson . . .

Don't wait even one day to start reinforcing students for following your classroom rules. As soon as the lesson has been taught, look for opportunities to recognize students for good behavior and immediately begin reinforcing students who follow the rules.

Let students know that you notice and appreciate the good efforts they're making. Through your actions, let them know that you mean what you said about supporting their efforts.

> "Jess, thank you for being in your seat before the bell rang."

These ideas will help support students' appropriate behavior at the start of the year.

Student Express Card

This activity works well with middle school students:

Give students some extra credit for their good efforts! Reproduce one "credit card" (page 83) for each student. During a designated time period, such as class discussion, ask students to leave their cards on their desks. Tell students that for the duration of the period (discussion, group work, lab work, etc.), you will be looking for students who are following directions and behaving responsibly. As you circulate the room, you can stamp or initial the cards of students who are behaving appropriately.

When all spaces on a student's card have been stamped or initialed, he or she turns in the card and earns a "You Deserve a Lot of Credit" reward coupon. These reproducible coupons (page 84) can be filled in by the teacher with a reward meaningful to the individual student.

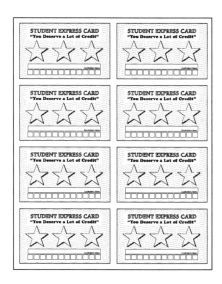

Great Start Raffle Tickets

Reinforce good habits by awarding Great Start Raffle Tickets to students who exhibit responsible behavior during the first weeks of school. When a student receives a ticket, he or she signs it, then deposits it in the class collection box. Once a week (or however often you determine), a designated number of tickets are drawn and prizes or privileges are given. This activity will motivate students to develop the responsible habits that will help them succeed all year long.

Try this: Encourage your students to start smart right at the start! Tell students that you will be awarding raffle tickets to those who return the signed discipline plan to school on time. Then hold a special drawing just for those students.

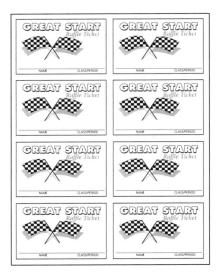

Students of the Week Bulletin Board

Recognize responsible behavior and effort all year long by putting the spotlight on different students each week. At the start of the year, explain that every week you will select one student from each class to be Student of the Week. The honor will include being highlighted on a Students of the Week Bulletin Board (students contribute photographs of themselves with family and friends), plus any special privilege or recognition you may wish to add.

Here's what to do:

1. Collect magazine covers or print selected covers from your computer to use as frames for student photographs. *People, Sports Illustrated, Rolling Stone, Newsweek,* and *Time* all make terrific backdrops for photos.

   The more eclectic a supply you gather, the more personalized your frames can be. (For example, a student who's a computer whiz would enjoy being placed on the cover of *PC World.* A budding rock musician would prefer *Rolling Stone.*) Cover the fronts of the magazines with construction paper, leaving just the mastheads showing.

2. Reproduce copies of the Student of the Week stars (page 86) on bright yellow or gold paper. Keep a supply handy so that each week you can write the name of each honored student in his or her own star.

3. Introduce the program to students, explaining that students who are selected as Student of the Week (on Friday) can bring photographs of themselves (with family and friends) to school on Monday to be displayed on the bulletin board.

4. Keep an instant camera at school to take pictures of any student who may not be able to contribute photographs.

5. Create the bulletin board by adding headline lettering: "Students of the Week." Each week add new photographs to the magazine frames and pin them up on the board with personalized stars.

Post rules reminders.

On pages 87–90, you will find posters of general rules that are commonly found in middle and secondary classrooms. If these rules are part of your plan, run them off on brightly colored paper (fluorescent or neon would get attention), or create your own version using computer-generated graphics, then display them in your classroom.

An open-ended bordered poster is also included to use for other rules of your own, as well as a Be Cool—Follow the Rules! poster (see page 92), which is applicable to any classroom.

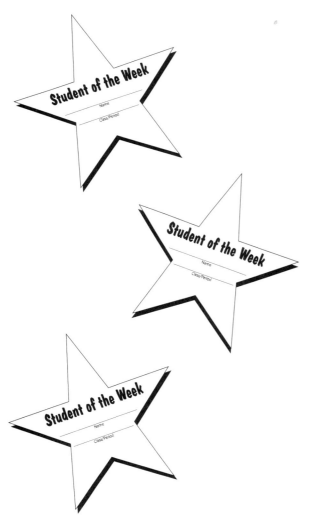

Post your plan.

Display the Rules, Supportive Feedback, and Corrective Actions posters in your classroom as an ever-present reminder of your classroom discipline plan. (This is important information for students, classroom visitors, new students, and substitutes, too.)

For the record . . .

Record your beginning-of-the-year classroom discipline plan lesson on an audiocassette or videocassette tape. When new students arrive in your classroom, they won't be at a disadvantage—they can see or hear that all-important lesson firsthand! Make sure that new students receive a copy of the classroom discipline plan letter to take home to parents (see page 95).

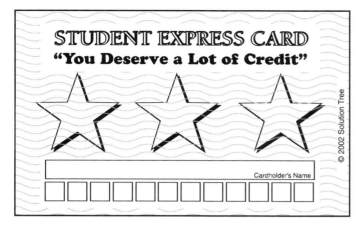

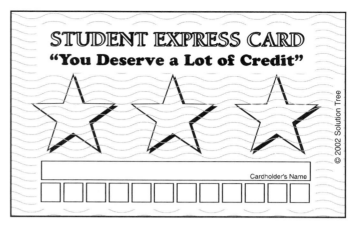

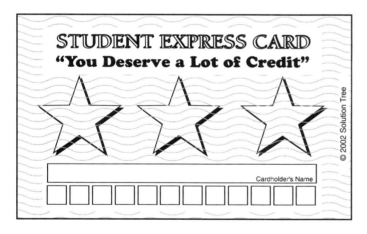

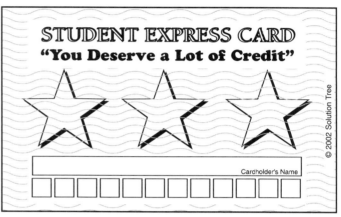

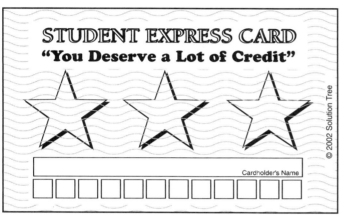

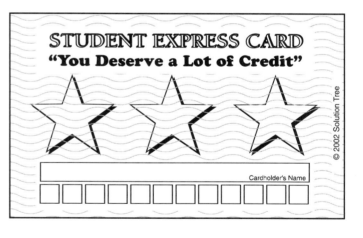

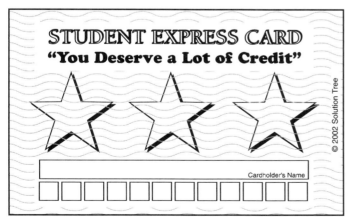

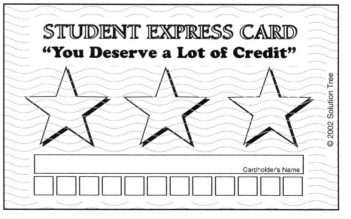

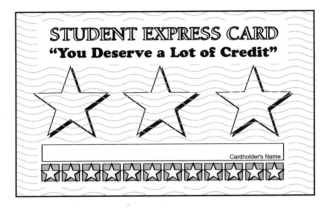

Congratulations on your super behavior!

This Student Express cardholder is entitled to

_____

_____

Signed	Date

© 2002 Solution Tree

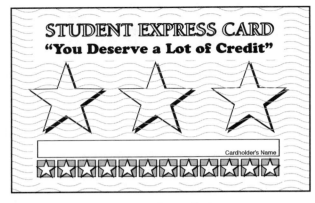

Congratulations on your super behavior!

This Student Express cardholder is entitled to

_____

_____

Signed	Date

© 2002 Solution Tree

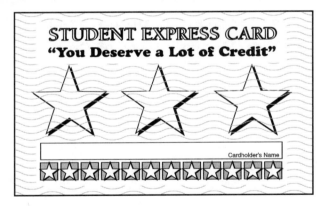

Congratulations on your super behavior!

This Student Express cardholder is entitled to

_____

_____

Signed	Date

© 2002 Solution Tree

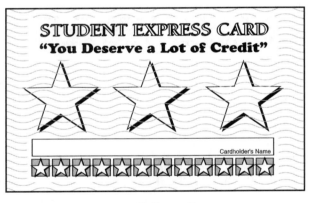

Congratulations on your super behavior!

This Student Express cardholder is entitled to

_____

_____

Signed	Date

© 2002 Solution Tree

NAME   CLASS/PERIOD

© 2002 Solution Tree

NAME   CLASS/PERIOD

© 2002 Solution Tree

NAME   CLASS/PERIOD

© 2002 Solution Tree

NAME   CLASS/PERIOD

© 2002 Solution Tree

NAME   CLASS/PERIOD

© 2002 Solution Tree

NAME   CLASS/PERIOD

© 2002 Solution Tree

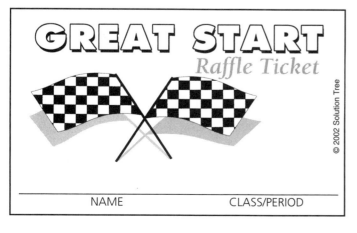

NAME   CLASS/PERIOD

© 2002 Solution Tree

NAME   CLASS/PERIOD

© 2002 Solution Tree

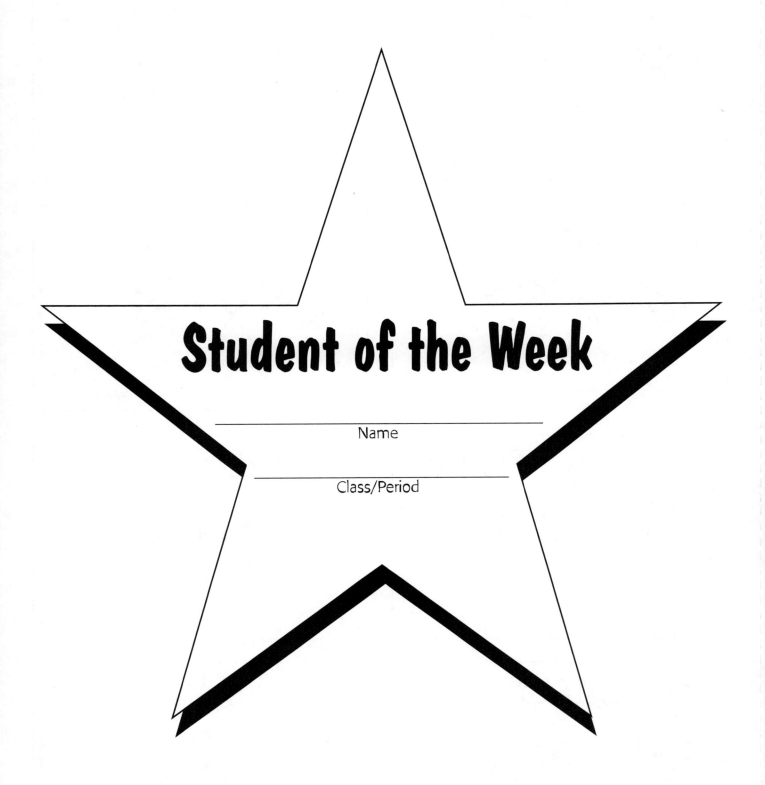

Student of the Week

_____
Name

_____
Class/Period

CLASSROOM
★ *Rule* ★

Follow directions.

CLASSROOM
★ *Rule* ★

Keep hands, feet, and objects to yourself.

CLASSROOM

★ *Rule* ★

Do not leave the room without permission.

CLASSROOM
★ *Rule* ★

Bring all required materials to class each day.

CLASSROOM

★ *Rule* ★

Be Cool— Follow the Rules!

Send Home a Copy of Your Classroom Discipline Plan to Parents

If parents are to become partners in their children's education, they must be well-informed about your classroom discipline plan. After all, contacting parents is part of your discipline hierarchy. You want them to be involved when you need them. Parents, therefore, need to be informed about why you have a plan and your rationale for rules, supportive feedback, and corrective actions.

Give each student a copy of your discipline plan to take home to parents. In an accompanying letter, explain why a classroom discipline plan is important, and ask parents to go over the plan with their child, sign the plan, and send it back to you.

Tell your students:

"Before you go home today, each of you will receive a copy of this letter to your parents. This letter explains our classroom discipline plan. I want all of you to talk with your parents about this plan. After you have talked about the plan, I want you and your parents to sign the bottom of the sheet. Please bring the tear-off portion back to me. I want all your parents to know what I expect of you in this class. And I want them to know that we will be working together to make sure this is a successful year for all of you."

Your letter to parents should include the following:

➤ Your reason for having a classroom discipline plan

➤ A list of the rules, supportive feedback, and corrective actions that are included in your plan

➤ A message asking parents to support your discipline plan

➤ An invitation for parents to call you with any concerns they might wish to discuss

➤ A tear-off sheet for parent signature and comments

It's Your Turn

Use the sample letter on page 95 as a guide to writing your own letter. It is recommended that you use your own words.

Word process the letter using your personal letterhead, or one designed for this purpose. Distribute the letters to students, keeping extras on file for new students who enter your class during the school year.

Substitute Support

There will be times when you won't be able to be at school (illness, meetings, etc.), but you can make sure that your classes continue to run smoothly and productively—no matter who is in charge. To ensure consistent behavior management in your classroom, even when you are not present, prepare a discipline plan for substitutes. Fill in your discipline plan on the substitute sheet on page 96. Make sure that a copy is left in the office. Put another copy in your lesson plan book or tape it to the top of your desk. If your plan is different in any respect for different classes, make sure you clearly note this. Stress to students that responsible behavior is expected when a substitute takes over—that the discipline plan is in effect no matter who is teaching.

It is also important that any paraprofessionals who work in your room understand the discipline plan and the role they are to play in its implementation. Take time to explain the plan.

CLASSROOM PLAN

Dear Parent:

I am delighted that your child _____ is in my (English, Geometry, History, Music, etc.) class this year. With encouragement, your child will participate in and enjoy many exciting and rewarding experiences this academic year.

Since lifelong success depends in part on learning to make responsible choices, I have developed a classroom discipline plan that guides every student to make good decisions about his or her behavior. Your child deserves the most positive educational climate possible for his or her growth, and I know that together we will make a difference in this process. The plan is outlined below.

Rules:
1. Follow directions.
2. Keep hands, feet, and objects to yourself.
3. No swearing, teasing, or name calling.
4. Be in your seat when the bell rings.

To encourage students to follow the rules, I will support appropriate behavior with verbal recognition, and positive notes and phone calls home.

However, if a student chooses to break a rule, the following steps will be taken:

First time a student breaks a rule:	Reminder
Second time:	Stay one minute after class
Third time:	Stay two minutes after class, and complete a Behavior Journal sheet
Fourth time:	Call parents
Fifth time:	Send to vice principal
Severe disruption:	Send to vice principal

Be assured that my goal is to work with you to ensure the success of your child this year. Please read and discuss this classroom plan with your child, then sign and return the form below. Don't hesitate to contact me if you have any questions about this plan or any other matter.

Sincerely,

_____

- -

I have read the discipline plan and have discussed it with my child, _____

_____

Parent/Guardian Signature   Date

_____

Student Signature   Date

Comments _____

_____

_____

SUBSTITUTE'S PLAN

From the desk of: _____

Dear Substitute:

Below are the guidelines for the discipline plan used in my classroom. My students know the rules. They understand that these rules are in effect at all times, and they know the corrective actions that will occur should they break the rules of the classroom.

Classroom Rules

1_____

2_____

3_____

4_____

Corrective Action

When a student breaks a rule:

1st time_____

2nd time_____

3rd time_____

4th time_____

5th time_____

Severe Clause: If a student exhibits severe misbehavior such as fighting or open defiance, or uses vulgar language, please do the following:

_____

_____

Please offer plenty of verbal reinforcement to students who follow the rules. They'll appreciate it, and your words of encouragement will help other students cooperate, too.

Thank you for following my classroom discipline plan.

Sincerely,

_____

Teaching Responsible Behavior

Developing your classroom discipline plan and teaching this plan to your students are the first steps you take to help them choose the responsible behavior that will enable them to succeed in school.

The next step is to teach your students how to make responsible behavioral choices in all situations at school.

In this section of the *Assertive Discipline Secondary Workbook,* we will look at a variety of techniques that will help you motivate the majority of your students to behave appropriately.

Also included in this section is a selection of reproducibles that will help you implement these techniques.

Determining and Teaching Specific Directions

Your classroom discipline plan lists the general rules in your classroom. As you have seen, these rules are in effect at all times.

The most important of these classroom rules is "Follow directions." This rule is included to ensure that students promptly follow any direction you might give during the class period.

To comply with this rule, students must understand what each specific direction you give means. You can never assume that a classroom full of students will follow a direction in the same way. After all, your students have five to seven teachers each day—each with different procedures and routines to follow.

➤ Do your students know how you expect them to participate during a class discussion?

➤ Do they know how you expect them to enter and leave the room?

➤ Do they know how you expect them to work together in groups?

There are many ways to go about following any direction. If you want all your students to follow a direction in the same way, you must teach them what you expect. Right at the beginning of the year, you need to take time to teach your students exactly how you want them to behave in all classroom situations. You need to teach and reteach your expectations until every student knows how to enter and leave the classroom, how to participate appropriately in a class discussion, and how to work in groups.

Remember, the goal is for all your students to succeed.

The more time you spend at the beginning of the year clarifying your specific directions, the less time you'll spend *repeating* them as the year goes by. Here's what to do:

First, identify the academic activities, routine procedures, and general policies for which specific directions are needed.

Next, determine the specific directions you want your students to follow for each activity and procedure you've identified.

Here are examples of academic activities:

➤ Teacher-directed lessons

➤ Group discussions

➤ Independent work

➤ Working in small groups

➤ Taking tests

➤ Making presentations to the class

➤ Working with computers and other technology

Here are examples of routine procedures:

➤ Entering the classroom

➤ Being dismissed from the classroom

➤ Collecting papers/homework

➤ Following an attention-getting signal

➤ Transitioning from one activity to another

➤ Taking attendance

➤ Viewing TV or video programs

Here are examples of general policies:

➤ Using the drinking fountain

➤ Using the pencil sharpener

➤ Using the restroom

➤ Care of desks, chairs, and other school property

➤ Use of computers

➤ Classroom interruptions (phone, visitors, etc.)

➤ Procedures for attending assemblies and special activities

➤ Emergency procedures

Note: Music, art, and PE teachers, and teachers who work in other special situations, should develop a list of the activities and procedures that apply to their students.

For example:

➤ Putting music equipment away

➤ Putting sports equipment away

➤ Cleaning up after an art activity

The Difference Between Rules and Directions

➤ **Rules** are posted in your classroom, and are in effect at all times during the day.

➤ **Directions** are in effect for the duration of a specific activity.

➤ **Directions** may change based on the teacher, the maturity level of the students, and the type of learning activity.

It's Your Turn

Now think about a typical week in your own classroom. Start at period one on Monday and work your way through to the end of the day on Friday. Identify the academic activities, routine procedures, and general policies your students will be engaged in. Try not to leave anything out. List all of these on a Specific Directions Worksheet (see page 100).

SPECIFIC DIRECTIONS
WORKSHEET

Use this worksheet to list all the instructional settings, routine procedures, and general policies that occur during the school week.

Academic Activities

- _____
- _____
- _____
- _____
- _____
- _____

- _____
- _____
- _____
- _____
- _____
- _____

Routine Procedures

- _____
- _____
- _____
- _____
- _____
- _____

- _____
- _____
- _____
- _____
- _____
- _____

General Policies

- _____
- _____
- _____
- _____
- _____
- _____

- _____
- _____
- _____
- _____
- _____
- _____

Now, determine the specific directions you want your students to follow.

After you've listed all the activities for which you need specific directions, it's time to decide on those directions. When determining the specific directions you want your students to follow, use these guidelines:

Keep it simple!

Choose a limited number of specific directions for each classroom activity.

Choose directions that are observable.

Your directions must be observable and easy for students to follow. Don't include vague directions such as "be good" or "behave appropriately."

Relate your directions to:

1. How you want students to participate in the activity or procedures—what you expect them to do

2. How you expect students to behave in order to be successful in the activity

Here are some examples of specific directions:

Academic Activity: Teacher-directed lesson in front of the class

1. Clear your desks of everything but notebook and pen or pencil.

2. Eyes on me, or eyes on your paper. No talking while I'm talking.

3. Raise your hand and wait to be called upon to ask or answer a question or make a comment. Don't shout out answers.

Academic Activity: Independent work

1. Have all necessary books, paper, pens, pencils, and other materials on your desk.

2. Begin working on your assignment as soon as you receive it.

3. No talking. Raise your hand to ask a question.

Routine Procedure: Entering the classroom

1. Walk into the room.

2. Go directly to your seat and sit down.

3. Take out your materials immediately.

4. No talking after the bell rings.

It's Your Turn

Write the specific directions for the classroom activities that apply to your own teaching situation. We've started the list with some activities that generally take place in all classrooms. Add to this list as needed.

Activity: When students enter the classroom

1_____

2_____

3_____

Activity: When you are instructing the class

1_____

2_____

3_____

Activity: When students are involved in a class discussion

1_____

2_____

3_____

Activity: When students are taking a test

1_____

2_____

3_____

Activity: When students turn in homework

1_____

2_____

3_____

Now write directions for any other classroom activities you listed on page 100.

Activity: _____

1 _____

2 _____

3 _____

Activity: _____

1 _____

2 _____

3 _____

Activity: _____

1 _____

2 _____

3 _____

Activity: _____

1 _____

2 _____

3 _____

Activity: _____

1 _____

2 _____

3 _____

Activity: _____

1 _____

2 _____

3 _____

Teach Your Specific Directions

Once you've determined your specific directions, your goal in teaching them is not to simply pass along instructions, but to make this process a learning experience for students as well.

Teach students *why* your directions are important to cooperation and successful learning. When students understand the reason behind your directions, they can take ownership of the expectations you hold for the class and will be better able to meet those expectations.

Why teach specific directions with such care?

Here are two good reasons:

➤ Teaching specific directions ensures that behavior problems will be reduced.

➤ Teaching specific directions assures greater academic success. Students know how to be successful during each activity. There is more time spent on task.

As with any successful lesson, preparation is vital to meeting your objectives. The lesson sequence that follows highlights points you'll want to include in your own specific directions lessons. Use this lesson as a guideline for developing a lesson for any specific direction. Keep in mind that your own lessons will differ, based on the age and maturity of your students and the direction you are teaching, but the focus on **explanation, teaching,** and **checking for understanding** remains the same.

Here's a sample lesson sequence for teaching specific directions for taking a quiz:

1. Explain the rationale for the directions.

Students need to understand why your directions are important. Explain why they need to follow these directions and what the benefit will be to them and to other students.

> "At the end of class each Friday, I will give the direction to get ready for a weekly quiz. It's important to follow directions so that you will be able to complete the quiz on time, and do well in this class."

2. Involve the students by asking questions.

Students will follow your directions more readily if you involve them in a discussion that rationally addresses your concerns.

> "What would happen if we wasted a lot of time getting ready for the quiz?"

3. Explain the specific directions.

Now teach the students the directions they are to follow. Remind them that when everyone follows these directions, all students will have an opportunity to succeed in class.

> "These are the directions you need to follow whenever I announce a quiz. When I say the words 'Friday quiz,' I want you to clear your desks, except for a pen. No talking. When you receive your quiz sheet, leave it facedown on your desk until I tell you to begin.

"When I say 'Begin,' turn your paper right-side up, write your name and the date, and begin taking the quiz. No talking. No getting out of your seat. If you have a question, raise your hand and I'll come over to you.

"When you're finished, check over your answers and turn the sheet over. You may take out a book and read silently until the papers are collected."

4. Check for understanding.
Check for understanding by asking students to restate the directions. Then reinforce the directions further by writing them on the board or presenting them on an overhead. At this point, you may also want to have students copy the specific directions to keep for reference.

After you've taught a specific directions lesson . . .

Immediately follow up any specific directions lesson with the activity or procedure that has just been taught. (In the previous example, the teacher would actually then give students the quiz.) Be sure to reinforce students who follow the directions appropriately, and give reminders (or reteach if necessary) to those students who don't.

First Two Weeks
Review directions each time the class engages in the activity.

First Month
Review directions each Monday (as a reminder and refresher for the week to come).

Remainder of Year
Review directions as needed. It is especially important to review directions after a vacation, or on special days when students are excited (the day before vacation, the day of a dance or major school event).

Here are some ideas that will help you teach specific directions to your students:

Plan your lessons.
Use the Lesson Plan for Teaching Specific Directions sheet on pages 107–108 to plan the lessons you will teach.

Post your directions.
Visual reminders can often help students remember directions. Create classroom posters of the most commonly given directions.

Create a Classroom Directions Binder.

As new students enter your class throughout the year, they too will need to learn your specific directions. This idea can ease their transition and involve peers in the teaching process:

Use the open-ended Lesson Plan for Teaching Specific Directions worksheet on pages 107–108 to create direction sheets for different activities.

Organize these sheets into a loose-leaf binder. When a new student joins the class, assign him or her a student guide. It's the responsibility of the guide to go through the binder with the new student and explain each of these directions.

The binder can also be used to reteach students who repeatedly receive warnings or corrective actions for not following directions. Have the student read and copy the specific directions he or she is having trouble with to help reinforce his or her understanding of the directions.

LESSON PLAN FOR TEACHING
SPECIFIC DIRECTIONS

Objective: To teach specific directions for _____

When to present this lesson: Teach directions for this activity prior to the first time the activity takes place.

These are the specific directions I will teach for this activity:

_____

_____

_____

_____

Now, plan the lesson you will teach.

Explain the rationale for the directions:

_____

_____

_____

_____

_____

_____

_____

_____

_____

_____

_____

_____

_____

_____

_____

Involve the students by asking questions:

_____

_____

_____

_____

_____

_____

_____

Explain the specific directions:

_____

_____

_____

_____

_____

_____

_____

_____

Check for understanding:

_____

_____

_____

_____

Notes on the lesson:

_____

_____

_____

_____

_____

_____

Using Supportive Feedback to Motivate Students to Behave

Once you've taught your students directions for all classroom activities, your goal is to help them be successful in following those directions.

Supportive feedback is the most effective way to achieve this goal.

We will give you a variety of techniques that you can use to motivate students to choose appropriate behavior and then to *continue* that behavior.

These techniques are:

1. Behavioral narration

2. Verbal recognition

3. Scanning

4. Circulating the classroom

On the following pages, you will learn how to use each of these techniques throughout the day—while you teach, and while you are involved in any classroom activity.

Keep Assertive Discipline in Action Cue Cards as Reminders

What are Assertive Discipline in Action Cue Cards?

Cue cards are a quick and easy way to keep Assertive Discipline techniques close at hand and in your mind. All of the supportive feedback techniques listed in this section, and other behavior management techniques included in the following section of this workbook, have been organized into easy-to-use Assertive Discipline in Action Cue Cards.

These reproducible cue cards give you portable, to-the-point references for successfully handling both appropriate and inappropriate classroom behavior.

Here are some guidelines for using cue cards:

➤ **Read them.**
Read each cue card. Think about how you can use each of these techniques in the day-to-day routine of your classroom.

➤ **Keep them.**
Laminate the cue cards and then tuck them into the back of your lesson plan book for easy reference. From time to time, review the techniques and make sure you are using them effectively and consistently.

➤ **Share them.**
Give a set of cue cards to your classroom aide or to parent volunteers. Encourage them to read the cards and use the techniques with students.

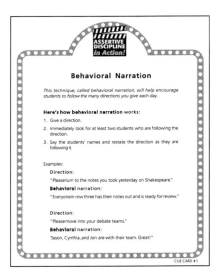

ASSERTIVE DISCIPLINE in Action!

Behavioral Narration

This technique, called behavioral narration, will help encourage students to follow the many directions you give each day.

Here's how behavioral narration works:

1. Give a direction.
2. Immediately look for at least two students who are following the direction.
3. Say the students' names and restate the direction as they are following it.

Examples:

Direction:
"Please turn to the notes you took yesterday on Shakespeare."
Behavioral narration:
"Everyone in row three has their notes out and is ready for review."

Direction:
"Please move into your debate teams."
Behavioral narration:
"Jason, Cynthia, and Jon are with their team. Great!"

CUE CARD #1

Behavioral Narration

This technique, called behavioral narration, will help encourage students to follow the many directions you give each day.

Here's how behavioral narration works:

1. Give a direction.
2. Immediately look for at least two students who are following the direction.
3. Say the students' names and restate the direction as they are following it.

Examples:

Direction:

"Please turn to the notes you took yesterday on Shakespeare."

Behavioral narration:

"Everyone in row three has their notes out and is ready for review."

Direction:

"Please move into your debate teams."

Behavioral narration:

"Jason, Cynthia, and Jon are with their team. Great!"

CUE CARD #1

Guidelines for Frequency of Behavioral Narration

At the beginning of the year, you will be placing a heavy emphasis on teaching students how to follow your classroom rules and directions. Thus, at the beginning of the year, you will use behavioral narration and other means of support much more frequently than you will once your students learn what you need them to do in each classroom situation. Remember, one of the goals of using supportive feedback is to start strong, then gradually decrease the frequency.

Weeks 1–2   Use behavioral narration every time you give a direction. Don't worry about overdoing it.

Weeks 2–4   Use behavioral narration every third time you give a direction.

After first month: Use behavioral narration every fourth or fifth time you give a direction. Maintain this frequency level throughout the year.

Behavioral narration is a positive advantage for you and your students!

You give hundreds of directions in a week. And each time you give a direction, you have a ready-made opportunity to acknowledge students. When you get into the habit of using this technique, you will be assured that you will make many more positive than negative statements to students.

Verbal Recognition

An effective way to encourage students to continue their appropriate behavior is to continually monitor the class—even while teaching—and provide frequent verbal recognition to those students who are on task.

Keep these guidelines in mind:

Verbal recognition is personal.

Always include the student's name. A statement like "Thank you for working quietly" is not as meaningful as "Teresa and Jackson, thank you for working quietly. Your cooperation is much appreciated."

Note: Remember that some adolescents do not respond well to praise given in front of their peers. With these students, it is best to deliver verbal recognition quietly after class or unobtrusively during a transition.

Verbal recognition must be genuine.

To be convincing to students, to show that you really mean what you say, be genuinely appreciative of their appropriate behavior.

Verbal recognition is descriptive and specific.

When acknowledging students, be specific. That way, students will know exactly what they did to deserve the recognition and will be more likely to repeat those behaviors. For example:

Descriptive Verbal Recognition	Vague Verbal Recognition
"Thanks, Shauntia, for an informative report."	"Good going, Shauntia."
"You must have really studied for this test, Mark."	"Nice job, Mark."
"Thank you for shutting down the computers, Sara."	"I like the way you're helping, Sara."

CUE CARD #2

Scanning

The scanning technique is useful when you are working with a small group of students, or an individual student, and the rest of the class is working independently. The objective of this technique is to reinforce students who are on task, thereby encouraging them to remain on task. This technique will help you recognize students who normally may not receive attention until they misbehave. By using this technique, you can keep independent workers on task and still work with one small group.

Here's how to use the scanning technique:

1. When you are working with a small group, look up every few minutes and scan the students who are working independently.

2. As you notice students who are working appropriately, take a moment to recognize their good behavior.

> "The group near the window has been working nonstop on the assignment. Thank you!"

3. The student will appreciate the recognition and continue working independently. Other students will get the message that you are aware of what's going on in the room, and will be motivated to stay on task themselves.

Note: Adolescents typically do not like to be singled out for praise in front of their peers. Praising a group of students, as in the example above, is far more effective.

CUE CARD #3

Circulating the Classroom

While students are working independently, circulate the room and give verbal recognition. One-on-one, you can let a student know that you recognize his or her appropriate behavior. This acknowledgment is given quietly—a special message from the teacher to the student.

"Shawn, this is going to be a terrific speech. The first line will really grab your audience."

"Maria, you've really been working hard all period, and your assignment is just about finished. Good work."

There is no need to ever phase out this technique. Each time you circulate the classroom, you have an opportunity to show your students you care, and that you notice their good efforts.

CUE CARD #4

Redirecting Nondisruptive Off-task Behavior

By teaching your rules and specific directions and by providing consistent positive support to your students, you can eliminate the majority of problems before they even begin.

Experience has perhaps shown you, however, that there will still be students who behave inappropriately. This behavior can take two forms: disruptive off-task behavior and nondisruptive off-task behavior.

Disruptive Off-task Behaviors

➤ Shouting out in class

➤ Throwing paper or other objects

➤ Pushing or shoving another student

➤ Slamming books on the desk

➤ Speaking disrespectfully to the teacher

Nondisruptive Off-task Behaviors

➤ Looking out the window

➤ Reading instead of listening

➤ Doodling instead of working

➤ Daydreaming

➤ Putting head on desk or sleeping

We will take a closer look at disruptive off-task behavior, and how to deal with it, on pages 122–123. Now we will focus on how to respond to nondisruptive off-task behavior—behavior in which a student is not disrupting others, but is not paying attention or staying on task, either.

As any teacher knows, students often fall into nondisruptive off-task behavior. They often lose focus and become inattentive to the work going on in the class. It doesn't take much for a 16-year-old to start doodling on his paper, or for a 13-year-old to lose interest in her class and begin to stare out the window.

The teacher's responsibility is to guide the student back into learning.

Here's what you *don't* want to do:

1. Ignore the behavior

2. Respond immediately with a corrective action

Ignoring the behavior doesn't get the student back on task, and therefore the student isn't participating or learning.

Using a corrective action, in many cases, is an overreaction to a simple lapse of attention.

Here's what you want to do:

Gently, and with caring guidance, give the student an opportunity to get back on task.

It's Your Turn

The Assertive Discipline in Action Cue Cards on pages 118–121 contain four techniques that will help you redirect a student's nondisruptive off-task behavior *while* you teach.

1. The "Look"

2. Physical Proximity

3. Mention Student's Name

4. Proximity Praise

Read each technique and imagine how you can use it throughout the day to nudge students back into your lessons. Reproduce these cue cards, laminate them, and keep them nearby for easy and frequent review.

Once a student is back on track . . .

As soon as a student is back on task, take advantage of the opportunity to verbally recognize his or her behavior. Let the student know that paying attention in class earns your positive attention.

How often do you redirect?

How many times should you redirect students before you start giving corrective actions? Obviously, you can't go on redirecting a student over and over within a class period. At some point, you may have to correct the student's actions.

Here's a rule of thumb:

When you find yourself having to redirect a student twice in a period, you can assume that the student is not receiving enough structure to help the student control his or her behavior. In these situations, turn to your discipline hierarchy and issue a reminder.

If the off-task behavior still continues, you may need to proceed to a further step on your discipline hierarchy.

> *Note:* If the off-task behavior still seems out of character for a student, perhaps there's something wrong. Before turning to your hierarchy, talk to the student and ask, for example, "It seems like it's hard for you to pay attention in class today. Would you like to talk about it?" Always remember that your own good judgment is your most valuable guide in assessing student behavior.

The "Look"

Just giving a look that says "I'm aware of and disapprove of your behavior" is an effective way of redirecting nondisruptive off-task behavior.

Here's how this technique works:

Instead of being actively engaged in the history lesson, Claudia sits aimlessly, tipping her chair back on two legs. When the teacher notices Claudia's off-task behavior, he makes direct eye contact with the student and looks at her with a firm, calm look on his face. The teacher maintains this eye contact until Claudia puts all four legs of her chair on the floor and begins to do the assignment.

CUE CARD #5

Physical Proximity

Sometimes you don't even have to say a word to redirect a student back on task. Simply walk over and stand close by the student. The student will know why you've arrived at his or her side and will respond.

Here's an example of physical proximity at work:

While introducing the next unit of chemistry curriculum, the teacher notices that Terry has put his head down on his desk and has tuned out. Continuing to speak, the teacher walks over to Terry's desk and stands there while proceeding with his introductory remarks. Terry becomes aware of the teacher's presence, lifts his head, and starts paying attention.

CUE CARD #6

Mention Student's Name

Just mentioning the off-task student's name while you are teaching a lesson may be enough to redirect his or her attention back on task.

Here's an example of a teacher using this technique:

While explaining a new mathematical concept, the teacher notices that Christina is off task and not paying attention. The teacher, in a matter-of-fact manner, continues the lesson, saying, "Now, I want all of you, including Christina, to work on a problem that uses this concept. Please open your math texts to page 84, and . . . "

As soon as Christina's name is mentioned, she looks up, tunes in, and immediately follows the direction.

CUE CARD #7

Proximity Praise

An effective way to redirect a nondisruptive off-task student back on task is to focus on the appropriate behavior of those students around him.

Here's an example of a teacher using proximity praise:

The entire class, with the exception of Jamie, is working independently on their research projects. Rather than doing his assignment, Jamie is doodling in his notebook. On either side of Jamie, Tawna and Colin are both doing their work. Wanting to get Jamie on task, the teacher says, "Tawna and Colin, you both look like you're really into your research. Keep up the good work."

As the teacher expects, Jamie looks around, notices what is going on, and gets back to work.

This technique is doubly effective. Off-task students are motivated to get back on task, and students who are on task receive well-deserved recognition.

CUE CARD #8

Implementing Corrective Actions

The previous techniques in this book will work to keep most students on task. However, when students disrupt and keep you from teaching, or other students from learning, you will have to follow through with the corrective actions you have proactively planned.

On page 62, you learned to develop a discipline hierarchy as part of your classroom discipline plan. How you use the hierarchy will determine its success in helping you motivate students to choose responsible behavior.

> *Remember:* Students need to learn that corrective actions are a natural outcome of misbehavior. The key is not the corrective action itself, but the inevitability that an action will be taken each time a rule is broken or a direction is not followed. Not sometimes, not every now and then, but every single time.

To successfully manage a classroom, there must be a balance between giving supportive feedback and providing corrective actions. Students will not respect your supportive feedback unless it is backed up with firm limits.

Follow these guidelines to ensure that your use of corrective actions will help students choose responsible behavior.

1. Provide corrective actions in a calm, matter-of-fact manner.

One of the benefits of a discipline hierarchy is that you always know how you will react to student misbehavior. Because you've planned how to deal with misbehavior, you will be able to follow through calmly, without anger, and with the assuredness that the corrective action is both appropriate and fair.

> "Tom, this is the second time I've had to speak to you about calling out in class. You have chosen to stay after class for two minutes."

2. Be consistent. Provide a corrective action every time a student chooses to disrupt.

As noted previously, it is the consistency of using corrective actions that is the key to their effectiveness.

3. After correcting a student's behavior, find the first opportunity you can to recognize positive behavior.

After a student has been disruptive, after the student has received a corrective action, teachers often begin to focus on that student's negative behavior—just waiting for that student to "act up" again. This may be a natural response, but it does little to encourage a student to choose more appropriate behavior.

Don't look for negative behavior. Instead, take the first opportunity to recognize the student's appropriate behavior. Your role in providing behavioral guidance (not punishment) to your students means that you must communicate the high expectations you have for each student's success.

Again, use discretion in how you recognize a student for appropriate behavior. Sometimes a simple smile or thumbs-up from across the room can convey as much as a verbal acknowledgment.

4. Provide an "escape mechanism" for students who are upset and want to talk about what happened.

After receiving a corrective action, students will often want you to stop what you are doing and listen to their side of the story.

The following "escape mechanism" will let students diffuse their anger and "get something off their chest," without disrupting the rest of the class:

➤ Have the student write you a note that you will discuss with him or her after class or when you have a break in the lesson.

➤ Use a notebook to record misbehavior that allows space for students to write their comments.

➤ Have students keep a daily journal or diary in which they can record any comments.

5. When a student continuously disrupts, "move in" or "move out."

There may be times when a student will continue to disrupt even after he or she has been given a reminder and a corrective action. In these situations, a technique called "moving in" (see Cue Card #9 on page 124) will often effectively stop disruptive behavior.

Keep in mind that by calmly and consistently implementing your discipline plan, you will help most students choose responsible behavior in your classroom. In spite of these efforts, however, there are going to be some cases in which students will challenge your authority and confront you. When a student tries to manipulate you or argue with you, you must stay in charge and refocus the conversation. Refer to the refocusing technique on Cue Card #10 (see page 125) for specific guidelines.

> Refer to *Assertive Discipline, 3rd Edition*, for further examples of effective uses of corrective actions.

"Moving In"

In many situations, physical proximity is all that is needed to help calm down a student and stop the disruptive behavior. Here's an effective technique to use when a student is being disruptive in class:

1. Move close to the student.

Walk over to the student. Get close. Show your concern and, in a quiet, firm manner, let the student know that his or her behavior is inappropriate.

2. In a caring manner, remind the student of the corrective actions taken so far, and what will happen next if the misbehavior continues.

"Monica, I am concerned that your behavior today is going to result in some corrective actions that you really don't want. You've been doing such a good job all week. I'm proud of the work you've done and I'd like to see it continue. Now, you're on the third step of the hierarchy. One more disruption and I will be calling your parents tonight. Do you understand?"

Note: Do not "move in" on more than one student at a time.

With some students, "move out."

With some students, it is more appropriate to "move out" of the classroom to speak to the student. With these students, removing the audience of peers may increase the effectiveness of your limit-setting efforts.

When you "move out," remember to:

- Stay calm.
- Avoid arguing with the student.
- Recognize the student's feelings.

Note: Do not "move" an older student out in front of the class. Either step outside or quietly move to the side of the classroom. It is important that these students save face.

CUE CARD #9

Refocusing an Argumentative Conversation

When a student starts arguing with you, you must stay in charge. Do not get involved in an argument. Do not let the student pull you into a pointless exchange. Instead, stay in control, refocus the conversation, and help get the student back on task.

Here's what to do:

- Stay calm.
- State what you want: "I want you to sit down and do your assignment."
- Preface your "statement of want" with understanding for the student.
- Repeat this statement a maximum of three times. If the student still argues, let her know that she may be choosing to receive a corrective action.

Here's an example of a teacher using the refocusing technique with a disruptive student:

Teacher:	*(calmly but firmly)* Rob, I want you to sit down and get to work on your assignment.
Rob:	It's almost done. I'll finish it tonight. I have to talk to Jack about our report for Mr. Ramos's class. We'll be quiet. We won't bother anyone.
Teacher:	I understand, Rob, but I want you to sit down and start your work for this class.
Rob:	But I need to talk to Jack. It's important. Why are you making such a big deal out of this?
Teacher:	Rob, I see that you're upset, but sit down and begin your work.
Rob:	I'm just trying to get my work done; it's due tomorrow.
Teacher:	Rob, if you don't get to work immediately, you and I will call your father during lunch. The choice is yours.

CUE CARD #10

Difficult Students

Consistent use of the classroom management skills presented in the first part of this workbook will enable most teachers to teach 90 to 95 percent of their students to choose responsible behavior.

The remaining 5 to 10 percent—the difficult students you sometimes encounter—are the focus of this section. We will cover four aspects of dealing successfully with difficult students:

➤ Build positive relationships

➤ Conduct one-on-one problem-solving conferences

➤ Develop an individualized behavior plan

➤ Gain support from parents and administrators

Build Positive Relationships

The adolescent years are stressful. Students' lives are filled with constant change as they leave childhood behind and experience the tumultuous physical, psychological, and social changes that mark the entry into adulthood.

The secondary teacher, therefore, fills a very special role in students' lives. Quite simply, the teacher is a guide through some of the most difficult years a young person will encounter. And for many students, their teachers are the most positive, caring role models they will have.

It is extremely important, then, that you make a special effort to establish positive relationships with difficult students—relationships that demonstrate your caring commitment to their success and well-being. Show these students that you care about them as unique individuals and that you are deeply concerned about their behavior.

In order to successfully raise the self-esteem of a difficult student, you may have to go beyond your daily program of positive support. Use special approaches and activities that enable you to reach out to those students on an individual basis to build strong, positive relationships.

It's as simple as this: Treat students the way you would want your own child to be treated in school.

It's Your Turn

The following pages contain ideas for fostering and building positive relationships with difficult students: a Student Interest Inventory, a Teacher Interest Inventory, and an Assertive Discipline in Action Cue Card detailing effective techniques to use with difficult students.

Discover Your Students' Interests

In order to establish personal relationships with your students, you need to learn about their likes and dislikes, interests, and goals. A Student Interest Inventory, taken at the beginning of the year, is a great way to learn more about each student. Explain to your students that this inventory will help you become better acquainted with each student. Make this inventory (see page 131) the first homework assignment of the year. Keep a supply of Student Interest Inventories on hand throughout the year to give to transfer students entering your classroom. The information you gather from this inventory could be the building blocks of a positive student/teacher relationship.

Turnabout is fair play!

Don't forget, students will want to know something about you, too. Create a Teacher Interest Inventory detailing your likes and dislikes, interests, and goals. Distribute a copy of the completed inventory to each student. Encourage students to discuss the inventory with you. Use the reproducible on page 132. Getting to know each other will help you build trusting relationships with students.

Don't hesitate to communicate!

A friendly note from a caring teacher can really make a student's day. Strengthen the positive support you give to your students, especially those who need extra guidance from you this year, with the reproducible notes on pages 133–135. Use them to express warm wishes to students or to share a few words of encouragement or appreciation. A bit of unexpected recognition can be the perfect booster students need to continue good efforts.

Look for opportunities each day to mail or hand out personalized notes to students. Customize your own notes using software programs of your own design, or any of the following notes:

Get-Well Note (page 133)

Being a teenager sick in bed is just not fun. Take a moment to brighten the day of an ailing student. Send home a get-well note to let the student know you are thinking about him or her and are looking forward to his or her return to class. Students will return to your classroom feeling a lot better—not only physically, but emotionally as well!

End-of-Term "Great Job!" Note (page 133)

Be sure that students leave your class with positive feelings about your class. At the end of the term or semester, fill in a note to recognize each student for a special quality, talent, or noteworthy contribution. Your favorable remarks will let students know that you care.

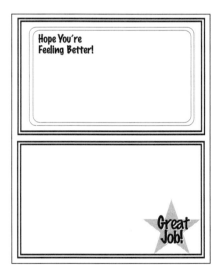

Thank-You Notes (page 134)

"Thank you!" They're just two little words, but they can mean so much. Use the thank-you notes to express appreciation to students for their help, cooperation, and thoughtfulness in class—or just to say thanks for being a great kid. Your thoughtfulness will be welcomed and appreciated.

Mid-Summer "Just Wanted to Stay in Touch" Letterhead (page 135)

By the end of the year, you will have worked hard all year long to help your students succeed academically and behaviorally. There are bound to be two or three students from each of your classes who would still benefit from your support and interest. Take the time to send a letter to these students just to let them know that you're thinking about them. Communicate the confidence you have in their future success.

Ideas for Building Positive Relationships

Build strong, positive relationships with difficult students by incorporating the simple yet effective techniques found on Assertive Discipline in Action Cue Card #11 (see page 136) into your daily routine. Keep this cue card handy as a reminder of the many ways you can make positive contact with all students, especially difficult ones, throughout the day. While many of the ideas are suitable for all your students, it is especially important to reach out to the most challenging ones. Those students may have come to your class with negative attitudes and distrust for adults. You will have to make a concerted effort to reach out to them to show you care.

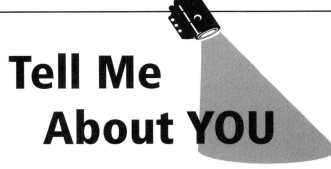

Tell Me About YOU

Welcome to my class! Getting to know you is important to me, and your answers to this survey will help. Your responses will be kept private, so please be honest. If you need more room to answer, use another sheet of paper or the back of this page.

Name: _____ Grade & Class: _____

Teacher: _____ Date: _____

Brothers and Sisters:

Name _____ Age _____

Name _____ Age _____

Name _____ Age _____

Name _____ Age _____

Special Friends: _____
_____

These are my favorite things to do: _____
_____

These are my favorites:

Book _____ Singer or group _____

Movie _____ Song _____

TV Show _____ Song _____

Some of the things that bug me are: _____
_____

I worry about: _____
_____

School would be better if: _____
_____

This is what a teacher did last year that I really liked: _____
_____

This is what a teacher did last year that bothered or upset me: _____
_____

One goal I'd like to accomplish this year: _____
_____

TEACHER INTEREST INVENTORY

Name _____

Family (optional):

Spouse _____

Children (ages) _____

Brothers and sisters _____

What I like to do most at home: _____

_____

_____

These are my favorite hobbies: _____

_____

_____

This is my favorite book: _____

This is my favorite TV show: _____

This is my favorite movie: _____

This is my favorite performer: _____

If I had one wish, I would want to: _____

_____

_____

What I like best about my students: _____

_____

_____

What I like best about teaching: _____

_____

_____

Why I became a teacher: _____

_____

_____

Hope You're Feeling Better!

Great Job!

Thanks!

Thank You!

Just wanted to stay in touch...

Ideas for
Building Positive Relationships

Greet your students at the door.

Start each day with a smile and a personal greeting—for each and every student. Stand at the door as your students enter the room and greet each student by name. "Good morning, Jamal. Nice to see you, Rebecca. Hi, George. Nice new jacket!" This is an especially effective way to make personal, positive contact with those students who need individual attention and caring words.

Spend a few special minutes with students who need your one-on-one attention.

The most precious and valuable gift you can give difficult students is your undivided attention. Take a few minutes during class, at recess, during lunch, or after school to talk to the student. Share information about yourself. Inquire about the student's feelings and concerns. Let that student know that you are there to offer assistance, understanding, and a sympathetic ear when necessary.

Make a phone call after a difficult day.

End a difficult day on a positive note by phoning a student with a positive message about tomorrow. Discuss any difficulties that occurred during the day. Get student input.

Most important, the phone call should emphasize your confidence that these problems can be worked through and that tomorrow, both of you can start fresh.

Make a positive phone call when a student has had a good day.

What better way to let a student know that he or she is on the right track than by making a quick phone call to offer some well-earned words of praise. If the student isn't home, share the good news with parents and have them deliver the positive message later.

Make get-well calls.

When a student is ill, pick up the phone and call to find out how the child is feeling. Both parents and student will appreciate your caring and concern.

Recognize a student's strengths and achievements, both academic and non-academic.

Look for areas in which a student shows particular strength (sports, music, art). Besides verbally recognizing the student's ability, find opportunities to engage the student to use his or her strength. (Invite the student to participate in a special school event. Suggest the student take part in designing a school mural.)

CUE CARD #11

Conduct One-on-One Problem-Solving Conferences

A one-on-one problem-solving conference is a meeting between you and a student to discuss a specific behavior problem. The goal of this conference is not to punish but to listen to the student and give caring and firm guidance. This conference should be looked upon as a cooperative effort on the student's behalf.

How do you know when a one-on-one conference is needed?

Ask yourself, "If this were my child, would I want her teacher to sit down and work with her to improve her behavior? Would I want her teacher to take time and interest to show my child options?"

If the answer is yes, then it is time to meet with the student.

Keep these guidelines in mind when conducting a one-on-one problem-solving conference:

1. Show empathy and concern.

First and foremost, let the student know that you are concerned and that you care about her. Let the student know that you are meeting not to punish but to help and offer guidance.

2. Question the student to find out why there is a problem.

Don't assume you know why the student is misbehaving. Ask questions.

"Did something happen to you today to get you so upset?"

"Are other students giving you a hard time?"

"Does the work in this class seem too difficult?"

"Is there something happening at home or in your neighborhood that concerns you?"

3. Determine what you can do to help.

Is there anything you can do to help solve the problem? There may in fact be a simple answer that you don't want to overlook.

For example:

➤ If a student is having trouble in class with another student, move his seat.

➤ If a disruptive student is seated at the back of the class, consider moving her forward.

➤ Contact the parents if you feel a student needs additional help and support from home.

➤ Increase your positive support of the student, not just your corrective actions. Look at the first praiseworthy behavior after the conference, then send a positive note home.

➤ A student may need academic help that you, a tutor, or a peer study buddy may be able to provide. Make that help available.

4. Determine how the student can improve his or her behavior.

Ask the student for his or her input concerning ways to improve the problem behavior. Share ideas. Keep in mind that students may not be willing or able to share their feelings about choosing a different behavior. If this is the case, help them by pointing out more appropriate behavior.

5. Agree on a course of action.

Combine your input with the student's input and agree upon a plan of action both of you can follow to improve the situation.

6. Clearly state that you expect the student to change his or her behavior.

At some point during the conference, you must let the student know that you expect the behavior to improve.

> "I'm going to work with you to solve this problem, Romario. You're a smart student, and I know you can behave responsibly. But you have to remember that while you're in this class, there is to be no teasing other students. Anytime you taunt or tease another student, you will be choosing to go to the assistant principal."

7. Summarize the conference. Show your confidence!

Wrap up the conference by summarizing what was said. Most important, end with a note of confidence.

> "I think we made a good start today, Romario. I know you can do better tomorrow. I'm glad we had this talk. If you ever feel like talking again, just let me know. I want this to be a good year for you."

Keep in mind that adolescents do not want to be told what to do. They want to feel they have a say in how they choose to behave. Whenever possible, involve the student in discussing how he or she should change behavior. Listen carefully to the student's input and give credence to his or her thoughts.

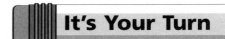

It's Your Turn

Use the Problem-Solving Conference Worksheet on the next page as a guide for conducting the conference and as a record of what was accomplished at the conference. If parents need to be involved at a future date, you will have documentation of steps already taken to solve the problem.

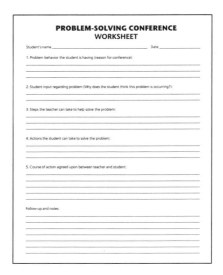

PROBLEM-SOLVING CONFERENCE
WORKSHEET

Student's name _____ Date _____

1. Problem behavior the student is having (reason for conference):

_____
_____
_____

2. Student input regarding problem (Why does the student think this problem is occurring?):

_____
_____

3. Steps the teacher can take to help solve the problem:

_____
_____
_____

4. Actions the student can take to solve the problem:

_____
_____
_____

5. Course of action agreed upon between teacher and student:

_____
_____
_____
_____
_____

Follow-up and notes:

_____
_____
_____
_____
_____
_____
_____

Develop an Individualized Behavior Plan

When your general classroom discipline plan is not effective with a student, you'll need to establish an individualized behavior plan for him or her. Such a plan is designed to adapt the concepts of your regular classroom discipline plan to meet the unique needs of a particular student.

An individualized behavior plan can help teach the student to behave responsibly and help you develop the positive relationship with that student that so far may have been out of reach.

An individualized behavior plan includes:

➤ The specific behaviors expected of the student

➤ Meaningful corrective actions to be imposed if the student does not choose to engage in the appropriate behavior.

➤ Meaningful supportive feedback to be given when the student does behave appropriately.

Guidelines for Developing an Individualized Behavior Plan

1. Determine the behavior(s) you expect from the student.

Select one or two behaviors to work on at a time. Choose those that you believe are most important to the student's success. For example, if a student has a consistent problem with staying in his or her seat, the rule "Stay in your seat unless you have permission to get up" would be an appropriate behavior to target.

2. Decide on meaningful corrective actions.

Often you will find that a difficult student reaches the same corrective action on the discipline hierarchy each day. For example, a student may reach the third step on the hierarchy every day and stay after class for two minutes on each of those days.

However, this student might always stop short of the corrective action that involves calling the parents. The teacher can conclude that it may be effective to individualize this student's discipline plan so that the first time he or she disrupts, instead of a reminder, instead of staying after class, the student's parents are called immediately.

Note: It may be appropriate with some difficult students to provide corrective actions that are not on your classroom discipline hierarchy. It may be necessary, for example, to keep a student in at lunch or after school even though the corrective action is not on your hierarchy.

Keep in mind that no matter what the corrective action is, it must always be one that will be meaningful to the student and, as always, provided consistently each time the student chooses to misbehave.

3. Determine more meaningful supportive feedback.

Your firmer, more meaningful corrective actions must always be balanced with increased supportive feedback. As always, begin with verbal recognition. Once you have implemented an individualized behavior plan, look for every opportunity to recognize the student's appropriate behavior. Make it a point to give positive attention to the student several times a day.

Back up your positive words with other forms of supportive feedback that you feel are appropriate, such as positive phone calls home or special privileges.

4. Keep parents informed.

A parent's involvement in an individualized behavior plan is critical. After all, it is likely that "call parents" may be the first corrective action you use. Whenever you establish an individualized plan for a student, personal contact with the parent is vital. A phone call or face-to-face meeting is your best means of communicating the plan.

Here are the points you will want to cover in the meeting:

➤ Emphasize to the parents that your goal in establishing the individualized plan is to help the student learn more responsible behavior that will allow him or her to succeed in school.

➤ Explain the one or two behaviors that you are dealing with in the plan. Let the parents know why you have chosen to emphasize these behaviors.

➤ Tell the parents what will happen the first time the student breaks one of these rules. Explain why you have chosen to use different corrective actions than those listed on the classroom discipline plan.

➤ Tell parents what will happen the second time a rule is broken.

➤ Ask if the parents have any questions regarding the use of the new corrective actions in the individualized plan.

➤ Explain the positive recognition you will give the student when he or she behaves appropriately. Reiterate the importance of reinforcing the student's efforts with consistent verbal recognition and other forms of support. Let the parents know that you are genuinely committed to the child's success.

➤ Tell the parents that you will provide a regular update to keep them informed of their child's progress. (In most cases, since parent contact will be part of the revised hierarchy, parents will hear if there's a problem. However, it's just as important to give a call or send a note when the student does behave appropriately.)

Emphasize the importance of parents following through at home with positive reinforcement of their own. If appropriate, give parents a copy of the student's individualized behavior plan.

Note: It is important that an individualized behavior plan be handled with sensitivity and caring. This is not a punitive effort; it is a plan tailor-made to meet a particular student's needs. Parents need to understand that this is a positive and proactive step, the goal of which is to help their child reach his or her potential. Let your words and attitude communicate this goal.

It's Your Turn

Use the Individualized Behavior Plan form on page 143 to help prepare and record a student's individualized plan.

The individualized behavior plan should be presented to the student in a firm but empathetic manner. Difficult students need your assurance that you care, that you are there to help, and that disruptive behavior is not in their best interest.

INDIVIDUALIZED BEHAVIOR PLAN

Student's name _____ Date _____

These are the rules that _____ is expected to follow as part of this Individualized Behavior Plan:

_____
_____
_____

These are the corrective actions _____ will choose to receive if he/she does not comply with the rule(s):

_____
_____

First disruption: _____
Second disruption: _____

This is the supportive feedback _____ will receive when he/she behaves appropriately:

_____
_____
_____

Teacher's signature _____ Date _____

Notes or comments:

_____
_____
_____
_____

Refer to *Assertive Discipline, 3rd Edition,* for more information on developing an individualized behavior plan.

INDIVIDUALIZED BEHAVIOR
PLAN

Student's name _____ Date _____

These are the rules that _____ is expected to follow as part of
this Individualized Behavior Plan:

_____

_____

_____

These are the corrective actions _____ will choose to receive if he/she does
not comply with the rule(s):

_____

_____

_____

    First disruption: _____

    Second disruption: _____

This is the supportive feedback _____ will receive when he/she behaves
appropriately:

_____

_____

_____

_____

_____

Teacher's signature   Date

Notes or comments:

_____

_____

_____

_____

_____

_____

_____

Gain Support from Parents and Administrators

In Section 1, you learned the importance of sharing your discipline plan with parents and with your administrator. These are important proactive measures that will help ensure that you get their support when you need it.

Keep these additional guidelines in mind as the year progresses and as behavior problems arise:

When a problem arises, take steps to deal with it on your own before asking for help.

Whenever appropriate, you should attempt to handle a student's disruptive behavior on your own before you speak to the parents or administrator about the situation. Both will want to know what actions you have taken to help the student. Assure them that you have already attempted to solve the problem on your own.

Remember, your goal is to teach the student to make good behavioral choices. If you involve parents or the administrator too soon, you are not allowing the student the opportunity to change his or her own behavior.

Document a student's behavior, and the steps you have taken to handle it.

When and if you do contact parents or an administrator, you will need accurate anecdotal documentation detailing when the problem has occurred and what steps you have taken to deal with it. Documentation strengthens your position as a professional and communicates clearly to parents that these problems do exist.

Your anecdotal record should include the following information:

➤ Student's name and class

➤ Date, time, and place of incident

➤ Description of the problem

➤ Actions taken by the teacher

For example:

Name: Justin Stern   Math 8

Date: _____

Problem: During math class, Justin twice grabbed Kerry's paper off her desk.

Actions taken: Moved Justin to the front of the classroom for period.

Keep these guidelines in mind when documenting problems:

Be specific. Keep away from vague opinions. Your statements should be based on factual, observable data.

Be consistent. Document problems each time they occur. Repeated occurrences may show a pattern and be helpful in solving the problem.

It's Your Turn

Use the reproducible documentation cards on page 146 to record anecdotal data about a student's behavior. Consider duplicating the cards on index stock for added durability. Fold them in half with the student's name facing forward. Or, use documentation spreadsheets on your computer and include the suggested information.

BEHAVIOR DOCUMENTATION CARDS

Student _____ Phone # _____
Parent's Name _____ Work # _____
Parent's Name _____ Work # _____

• Date _____ Time _____ Place _____
Description of Problem/Incident: _____

Action Taken: _____

• Date _____ Time _____ Place _____
Description of Problem/Incident: _____

Action Taken: _____

• Date _____ Time _____ Place _____
Description of Problem/Incident: _____

Action Taken: _____

• Date _____ Time _____ Place _____
Description of Problem/Incident: _____

Action Taken: _____

Student _____ Phone # _____
Parent's Name _____ Work # _____
Parent's Name _____ Work # _____

• Date _____ Time _____ Place _____
Description of Problem/Incident: _____

Action Taken: _____

• Date _____ Time _____ Place _____
Description of Problem/Incident: _____

Action Taken: _____

• Date _____ Time _____ Place _____
Description of Problem/Incident: _____

Action Taken: _____

• Date _____ Time _____ Place _____
Description of Problem/Incident: _____

Action Taken: _____

BEHAVIOR DOCUMENTATION CARDS

Student _____ Phone # _____

Parent's Name _____ Work # _____

Parent's Name _____ Work # _____

• **Date** _____ Time _____ Place _____

Description of Problem/Incident: _____

_____

Action Taken: _____

_____

• **Date** _____ Time _____ Place _____

Description of Problem/Incident: _____

_____

Action Taken: _____

_____

• **Date** _____ Time _____ Place _____

Description of Problem/Incident: _____

_____

Action Taken: _____

_____

• **Date** _____ Time _____ Place _____

Description of Problem/Incident: _____

_____

Action Taken: _____

_____

FOLD HERE

Student _____ Phone # _____

Parent's Name _____ Work # _____

Parent's Name _____ Work # _____

• **Date** _____ Time _____ Place _____

Description of Problem/Incident: _____

_____

Action Taken: _____

_____

• **Date** _____ Time _____ Place _____

Description of Problem/Incident: _____

_____

Action Taken: _____

_____

• **Date** _____ Time _____ Place _____

Description of Problem/Incident: _____

_____

Action Taken: _____

_____

• **Date** _____ Time _____ Place _____

Description of Problem/Incident: _____

_____

Action Taken: _____

_____

Getting Support from Parents When a Problem Arises

How do you know when you should contact a parent about a problem? Some situations are very clear: severe fighting, extreme emotional distress, or a student who refuses to work or turn in homework. Don't think twice about involving parents when these situations occur.

What about the day-to-day instances that may not be so obvious? If you are uncertain about contacting a parent, use the "Your Own Child" test. This test will put you in the position of the parent, and help clarify whether or not parental help is called for.

The "Your Own Child" Test

1. Assume you have a child of your own the same age as the student in question.

2. If your child were having the same problem in school as that student, would you want to be called?

3. If the answer is yes, call the parent. If the answer is no, do not call the parent.

Before you pick up a phone or meet with parents, you need to outline what you are going to say. These notes will help you think through and clarify the points you want to make. Having the notes in front of you while you're speaking will help you communicate more effectively.

It's Your Turn

Assertive Discipline in Action Cue Card #12 (see page 148) lists all the points you'll want to cover when contacting a parent about a problem. Reproduce and laminate this cue card and keep it available for use. Use the reproducible Parent Contact Worksheet on page 149 to help you prepare for your meeting and to record pertinent data from the meeting.

Contacting Parents About a Problem

Follow these steps when contacting a parent about a problem:

1. **Begin with a statement of concern.**

   Let the parent know that you care about the student.

2. **Describe the specific problem and present pertinent documentation.**

   Explain in specific, observable terms what the student did.

3. **Describe what you have done.**

   Explain exactly how you have dealt with the problem so far. Make sure that the parent is aware of the steps you have already taken to solve the problem.

4. **Get parental input on the problem.**

   Listen carefully to what the parent has to say. Here are some questions you may want to ask:

   "Has your child had similar problems in the past?"

   "Why do you feel your child is having these problems at school?"

   "Is there something (divorce, separation, siblings, a move) going on at home that could be affecting your child's behavior?"

5. **Get parental input on how to solve the problem.**

   Parents may have a good idea that could help solve a specific problem. Ask for input, and listen carefully to the responses.

6. **Tell the parent what you will do to help solve the problem.**

   You've already explained what you have previously done. Let the parent know exactly what specific actions you are going to take now.

7. **Explain what you need the parent to do to solve the problem.**

   Clearly and carefully explain specifically what you would like the parent to do.

8. **Let the parent know you are confident that the problem can be worked out.**

   Wrap up the conversation or meeting on a positive note.

9. **Tell the parent that there will be follow-up contact from you.**

   The parent needs to know that you are going to stay involved. Provide this reassurance by giving a specific date for a follow-up call or note.

10. **Recap the conference.**

    Clarify all agreements. Restate or write down what you are going to do and what the parent is going to do. Keep this information in your files.

CUE CARD #12

PARENT CONTACT
WORKSHEET

Student's name _____ Date of call or meeting _____

Parent or guardian _____

Home phone # _____ Work phone # _____

In the spaces below, write the important points you will cover with the parent, and points made during the meeting or conversation.

1. Begin with a statement of concern. _____
_____

2. Describe the specific problem (state in observable terms). _____
_____

3. Review what you have already done to solve the problem. _____
_____

4. Get parental input on how to solve the problem. Record parent comments. _____
_____

5. Present your solutions to the problem.

What you will do: _____
_____

What you want the parent to do: _____
_____

6. Express confidence once again in your ability to solve the problem.

7. Arrange for follow-up contact.

Notes: _____
_____
_____
_____
_____

Make the Most of Your Professional Development Investment

Let Solution Tree (formerly National Educational Service) schedule time for you and your staff with leading practitioners in the areas of:

- **Professional Learning Communities** with Richard DuFour, Robert Eaker, Rebecca DuFour, and associates
- **Effective Schools** with associates of Larry Lezotte
- **Assessment *for* Learning** with Rick Stiggins and associates
- **Crisis Management and Response** with Cheri Lovre
- **Classroom Management** with Lee Canter and associates
- **Discipline With Dignity** with Richard Curwin and Allen Mendler
- **PASSport to Success** (parental involvement) with Vickie Burt
- **Peacemakers** (violence prevention) with Jeremy Shapiro

Additional presentations are available in the following areas:

- At-Risk Youth Issues
- Bullying Prevention/Teasing and Harassment
- Team Building and Collaborative Teams
- Data Collection and Analysis
- Embracing Diversity
- Literacy Development
- Motivating Techniques for Staff and Students

Solution Tree

304 West Kirkwood Avenue
Bloomington, IN 47404-5131
(812) 336-7700
(800) 733-6786 (toll-free)
FAX (812) 336-7790
e-mail: info@solution-tree.com
www.solution-tree.com

NEED MORE COPIES OR ADDITIONAL RESOURCES ON THIS TOPIC?

Need more copies of this book? Want your own copy? Need additional resources on this topic? If so, you can order additional materials by using this form or by calling us toll free at (800) 733-6786 or (812) 336-7700. Or you can order by FAX at (812) 336-7790, or visit our web site at www.solution-tree.com.

Title	Price*	Quantity	Total
Assertive Discipline® Secondary Workbook Grades 6–12	$ 11.95		
Assertive Discipline® Elementary Workbook Grades K–6	11.95		
Assertive Discipline®: Positive Behavior Management for Today's Classroom, 3rd Ed.	19.95		
Assertive Discipline® (staff development video set)	495.00		
Lee Canter's Classroom Management for Academic Success	39.95		
First-Class Teacher: Success Strategies for New Teachers	22.95		
Succeeding With Difficult Students	17.95		
Succeeding With Difficult Students (staff development video set)	495.00		
Teaching Students to Get Along	17.95		
Teaching Students to Get Along (staff development video set)	395.00		
Teacher's Plan Book Plus #1: Assertive Discipline®	9.95		
Teacher's Plan Book Plus #2: Assertive Discipline®	9.95		
Lee Canter's Record Book Plus	9.95		
SUBTOTAL			
SHIPPING Please add 6% of order total. For orders outside the continental U.S., please add 8% of order total.			
HANDLING Please add $4. For orders outside the continental U.S., please add $6.			
TOTAL (U.S. funds)			

*Price subject to change without notice.

❏ Check enclosed   ❏ Purchase order enclosed
❏ Money order   ❏ VISA, MasterCard, Discover, or American Express (circle one)

Credit Card No._____ Exp. Date _____

Cardholder Signature _____

SHIP TO:

First Name_____ Last Name_____

Position_____

Institution Name_____

Address_____

City_____ State_____ ZIP _____

Phone_____ FAX _____

E-mail _____

Solution Tree (formerly National Educational Service)
304 West Kirkwood Avenue
Bloomington, IN 47404-5131
(812) 336-7700 • (800) 733-6786 (toll-free number)
FAX (812) 336-7790
e-mail: orders@solution-tree.com • www.solution-tree.com